Care of Australian Wildlife

Care of
AUSTRALIAN WILDLIFE

For Gardeners, Landholders and Wildlife Carers

REVISED EDITION

Erna Walraven

Illustrations by Rebecca Hale

This updated edition published in 2023 by
New Holland Publishers
Sydney

Level 1, 178 Fox Valley Road, Wahroonga, NSW 2076, Australia

First published in 1999
Revised and reprinted in 2004
Reprinted in 2010

Printed in China

10 9 8 7 6 5 4 3 2 1

ISBN 978 1 92107 373 1

Managing Director: Fiona Schultz
Publisher: Simon Papps
Illustrations: Rebecca Hale
Production Director: Arlene Gippert
Designer: Jo Waite
Cover Design: Andrew Davies

Other New Holland books by Erna Walraven:

WILD LEADERSHIP
What Wild Animals Teach Us About Leadership
ISBN 978 1 92554 635 4

WILD FATHERS
What Wild Animal Dads Teach Us About Fatherhood
ISBN 978 1 92554 672 9

For details of hundreds of other Natural History titles see newhollandpublishers.com

 Keep up with Reed New Holland and New Holland Publishers on Facebook at
ReedNewHolland and NewHollandPublishers

Lizards enjoy basking in the sun; they use the sun's energy to warm up their bodies.

Foreword

For many people their only involvement with wildlife is their contact with the few species that have managed to co-exist with the urban sprawl. People may have this contact in their gardens, on their balconies or as they walk in the small patches of remnant vegetation or bushland isolated by the burgeoning human population. These 'islands' of habitat are eventually unable to sustain the plants and animals that existed there originally and become mere shadows of their former selves. Our record in relation to animal and plant extinction is one of which we should be ashamed and it behoves us all to try to assist where we can to resolve, or at least arrest, this species decline.

When people want an 'animal experience' they often think of fauna parks and zoos and will come to see the animals, large and small, which are exhibited for their benefit and education within the zoo proper. It is important that large numbers of people do visit our zoos for recreation—it is revenue raised from this source which, to a large extent, assists zoos to fund the conservation work that they undertake.

Within many zoos throughout Australia, another area to which these 'leisure dollars' are applied is to the care and rehabilitation of injured wildlife. Many of the animals, after a short sojourn in care, are returned to the wild. Unfortunately some of the animals rescued are too badly injured to survive. Others may not be fit enough to return to the wild and are used in education programs within the zoo.

We are singularly fortunate that Erna Walraven, who has vast experience in the care of wildlife, both in zoos and in nature, has decided to document her expertise. This book gives simple, clear guidelines about caring for our wildlife, both plant and animal, together with suggestions on how to avoid future problems.

I congratulate both Erna Walraven and Rebecca Hale on the high standard of the text and illustrations. I am confident that this book will form a compulsory part of the library of many people across Australia in city, town and country, and will be of great assistance in maintaining our wildlife. I commend it to you.

Ed McAlister OA BSc JP,
Former President,
World Association of Zoos and Aquariums

Preface

One of the most perplexing problems that the Australian urban dweller faces is how to deal with the conflict between wildlife and the development of our cities and towns. The habitats of many native species have been so dramatically changed by humans that they are now completely hostile to their continued survival. Loss of native vegetation, threats from our domestic animals, introduced wild species, the dangers of our technology and machines—the list seems endless. Yet, amazingly, many species survive.

The desire to improve this situation leads us to ask many questions: how do we provide relatively natural and secure surroundings and proper sources of food and protection from introduced predators? How do we handle sick and injured wildlife? The urban dweller often has little experience and few answers to these dilemmas.

It is timely, therefore, that Erna Walraven has prepared a new edition of this extremely useful, readable and practical book. *Care of Australian Wildlife* is essential reading for the many Australians interested in wildlife, particularly those who feel that they can do something to improve the lot of our native species which are so commonly disadvantaged by our urban way of life.

Dr David Butcher
Former Chief Executive
World Wide Fund for Nature
Australia

Acknowledgements

Over the years the dedication of zoo staff has contributed to the build-up of current knowledge of our wildlife and its needs. There are too many past and present zoo colleagues and friends to mention but I would like to acknowledge their contribution to current wildlife husbandry practices.

Recognition is particularly due to the following individuals for their generous support and contributions, critical appraisals and many helpful suggestions: Lesley Reddacliff, Dedee Woodside, Derek Spielman, Dave Robson, Graeme Phipps, Laura Mumaw, Teri Bellamy, Ian Fry, Terry Boylan, David Pepper-Edwards, Annette Gifford, Chris Hibbard, Libby Hall and Wayne Boardman.

Rebecca Hale drew the informative and delightful line illustrations that accompany the text. I am also grateful to Don Dick whose knowledge of the English language contributed to the original publication on this topic.

Finally, many, many thanks to Rob, who has put up with a fridge full of cockroaches, fly pupae, mealworms and much worse.

Contents

FOREWORD   vi

PREFACE   vii

ACKNOWLEDGEMENTS   viii

GALAH BY DAVID MCK BERMAN   xi

1   WILDLIFE AND THE ENVIRONMENT   1

2   FOOD AND SHELTER   12

3   CASE STUDIES: ENCOUNTERS WITH WILDLIFE   37

4   EMERGENCIES—WHAT TO DO   51

5   HANDLING AND EMERGENCY CARE FOR COMMON
       MAMMAL GROUPS   62

6   HANDLING AND EMERGENCY CARE FOR
       COMMON BIRD GROUPS   75

7   HANDLING AND EMERGENCY CARE OF REPTILES   91

8   HAND-REARING ORPHANS   99

Appendix 1: WILDLIFE AUTHORITIES   127

Appendix 2: PRODUCTS AND MANUFACTURERS   129

Appendix 3: FURTHER ACTION—CONSERVATION GROUPS   130

INDEX   133

Galah

I was a little pink galah
Just sitting on the highway tar,
Just sitting, eating on the road
Wheat that spilt from someone's load,
Fighting for the finest seed
Disgusted with my partner's greed,
Then flying high to miss the cars
Which often flatten slow galahs,
Then landing on the road once more
To get the wheat we'd missed before.

Just then I found a lovely grain
It made the other wheat look plain
It was big and rounded but
It had fallen in a rut
My friends were squawking,
'There's a car,
Get off the road ya mad galah!'
I didn't fly, I'd just about
Got that delicious seed dug out,
My friends were making quite a fuss
Squawking that 'The car's a bus!'

I got the seed an' flew but splat
And now I'm feeling rather flat
A very sore and sorry bird,
The driver hadn't even heard
And here I am stuck on the grill
Feeling quite a dopey dill,
But not everyone can poach
A ride upon a tourist coach
And as I drive about today
I see the world a different way.

Life's not only piles of grain
Sprinkled there like golden rain
There's other things along the road,
A dead wombat and flattened toad,
And there's a mangled kangaroo
A victim of the highway too,
A blue-tongue lizard thought it great
To lie and thermoregulate
In the middle of the road
But he's squashed there like the toad.

The wombat with his tiny stride
Ran but found the road too wide,
The roo had some grass to munch,
Saw the lights, hopped then crunch,
Now eating them's some hawks and crows
There's never any dead of those
And up here on the grill with me
There's moths and hoppers and a bee,
A butter and a dragonfly,
The highway caused them all to die.

So all of you who use the road,
Drive a car or spill a load,
Or fly towards bright headlights
Or hop across the road at nights
Or lie there baking in the sun
Or run across the road for fun
Or eat the grass along the side
Just think of all of us who've died.

from *Dead Pegs* by
David McK Berman,
Bandicoot Books, Australia, 1987

Wildlife AND THE ENVIRONMENT?

We all have a role to play in protecting our precious wildlife. No-one would argue that many animals are successfully conserved in national parks and reserves. However, only a small portion of the country is officially devoted to the conservation and protection of wildlife in such areas. The number of animals protected in national parks is only a fraction of the number of native animals that need protecting. Many more species could be saved from extinction, and more individual animals could be saved from local extinction, if the community played a bigger role in wildlife conservation. More could be achieved if conservative land-use practices were applied over the entire country, including multiple land-use functions that consider the needs of wildlife and the interests of the community.

Land clearing in Australia has had many negative effects, such as salination, rising watertables and erosion. Such effects cost the rural community and Australia a great deal of money and could largely be avoided if clearing was more selective. With careful management and planning, suitable habitats could be preserved to cater for both wildlife and human needs.

Many animals cannot be maintained in restricted areas. They are migratory or nomadic and need to travel for breeding or simply to find sufficient food and water. Without the interchange of genetic material, inbreeding can occur. This increases the likelihood of local extinction unless new individuals enter the population. Migration, particularly for mammals, is often dangerous as many populations are separated by major roads and urban developments. Wildlife corridors link some reserves and isolated populations, but many more are needed.

Urban wildlife corridors can be created by planting native vegetation on railway reserves, nature strips along powerlines, easements for stormwater drains and in local recreation parks. Residential gardens can also make up a network of interlocking wildlife corridors. We can all improve our backyards and home paddocks to support wildlife and, at the same time, make the environment more attractive for ourselves. Gardens, parks, school grounds, nature strips and clubhouse environments can all be developed to provide suitable habitats for local wildlife. Every small addition to a growing network of wildlife corridors is a step forward for wildlife. It also beautifies the environment for all to enjoy.

By making your garden a sanctuary for wildlife, it may become an important link for migratory or nomadic birds travelling between their resource areas as well as providing essentials for other resident animals.

What is wildlife?

Wildlife includes all non-domestic plants and animals. In a typical urban backyard, the kinds of animals to be found may be birds, such as honeyeaters and wrens, native mammals, such as possums and gliders, and garden skinks and other lizards, plus bees, spiders, ants, worms and many, many more. Some of these animals are clearly visible, for example, birds feeding in a tree or in the garden, or skinks that scatter every time you walk out on a sunny day. Others may be more secretive, for example, a resident possum may not be noticed until it decides to move into your roofspace as a temporary abode.

Wildlife also includes plants. This book does not address the specific issue of plant care; it treats plants more collectively as 'habitat' for animals, and encourages ways of restoring and retaining a suitable habitat. The appropriate habitat automatically caters for a myriad

of life forms. Plants and animals evolved together and are largely interdependent—the continued survival of one requires the presence of the other.

It is much easier to become concerned about the survival of lorikeets which visit the garden than to take an interest in a rare and endangered plant that you have never seen before. However, to ensure the long-term existence of native animals, we must give them somewhere to live and protect all natural life forms within that system, including vegetation, soil organisms, insects and fungi. In an effort to conserve wildlife—that is, preserve it for the future— the first and most important step is to understand the interrelationships existing in our own backyards.

What is a habitat?

A habitat is the place where a creature normally lives. For an animal, its habitat has everything it needs, such as food, water, a safe place to rest and sleep and the potential to find a mate so that it can reproduce. Just as a species can be identified by the way it looks, so can its habitat be defined.

There are many types of habitat, each important to the animals that live there. In Australia there are rainforests, forests, woodlands, scrubland, grasslands, heathlands, mangroves, wetlands and deserts. Each of these environments supports an array of different wildlife species. The animals, in turn, impact positively on their environment in many ways. They disperse seeds and pollinate plants. Predators and prey balance each

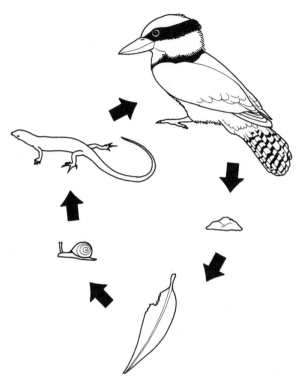

An example of a simple food chain: kookaburra droppings provide nutrients for the vegetation to grow; the vegetation is eaten by the snail; the snail is eaten by the lizard; the lizard is eaten by the kookaburra.

other's population numbers and scavengers clean up carcasses. Animals also help control pests and their faeces fertilise the soil.

Conservation of habitat is therefore an essential part of wildlife conservation. We must look after an animal's habitat if we want to conserve the species. Studies have shown that the differences in the number of animal species in habitats is related to the number of vegetation layers. If the vegetation has many layers, such as tall trees, medium-sized trees, shrubs, bushes, grasses and ground cover, various species are able to use the different levels. Usually a variety of vegetation layers also means a greater diversity of food is available to wildlife. More complex habitats can generally support more species than less complex habitats.

What does wildlife need to survive?

Every plant and animal has a set of minimum requirements in order to survive. The obvious requirements are shelter, food, water, air and protection. Others may be more specific—for example, Welcome Swallows need mud to build their nests while many birds, such as honeyeaters, fantails and Willie Wagtails, find spider webs an essential component of a suitable nest.

Even if only one of these requirements is missing, the animal or group of animals cannot live successfully in the area and this will limit the species' survival in the long term. This is called a limiting factor.

Do you know why Koalas were sometimes referred to as 'bears'?

European scientists first described the Koala as an 'ash-coloured pouched bear' (*Phascolarctos cinereus*) and farmers used to call them native bears. The Koala is a unique Australian animal and is not related to bears at all. The correct name is Koala.

You may remember native animals that were common in your urban area 10 or 20 years ago but are now rarely seen. Some of these species may be encouraged to return if we can identify all of their essential needs. Several species of bandicoot, for example, were common in suburban backyards not many years ago but have now virtually disappeared from urban areas, except in a few strongholds in larger nature reserves. The critical or limiting factor in the bandicoot's case was probably predators—domestic and feral cats and dogs. Add to this the decrease in shelter through loss of dense undergrowth and the bandicoot had no protection and no home sites. Direct extermination has also been responsible.

In many gardens, bandicoots have been trapped, poisoned and destroyed for digging up lawns or they have been mistaken for rats.

Once we determine the limiting factors, we can set out to provide the minimum essential needs for wildlife and hope that they will respond and adjust to the changed environment.

Safety for wildlife

In Australia we have about 30 species of well-established introduced animals. These include buffalo, camels, rabbits, pigs, goats, horses, donkeys, foxes, dogs, cats, European bees, sparrows, Indian Mynas and many more. The impact of these animals on the natural environment and on native wildlife is devastating. They compete with native animals for nesting sites and food. Predation by introduced animals on native species is also very high. In addition, the behaviour of some introduced animals can upset the balance of nature. For example, the wallowing of pigs and buffalo can alter the natural environment to such an extent that it becomes unsuitable for the native animals.

The introduced species that exist in the urban environment include dogs, cats, foxes and a variety of introduced birds, such as the common pigeon, starling, sparrow, blackbird and Indian Myna. Introduced birds create problems for native birds and some small mammals by competing for resources such as food and nesting sites. Birds such as Indian Mynas are far more aggressive than most native bird species and chase the small native birds away from food sources and nesting sites. Introduced birds thus contribute to the decline of small native birds in urban areas. Fortunately, most introduced birds have not been able to establish themselves in the bush and are mainly restricted to an urban environment. The common starling and Indian Myna prefer lawn and garden parks. Their presence can be discouraged by planting the garden with habitat plants for native species and by not feeding them.

The existence of introduced predators such as cats, dogs and foxes is a very serious problem for ground-dwelling animals like quails, bandicoots and native rodents. Many arboreal (tree-dwelling) animals, such as possums and gliders, also fall prey to introduced predators because the loss of suitable habitat forces them to spend more time on the ground. When the distance between big trees does not allow the arboreal animals to jump from one tree to the other they must get there by coming to the ground where they are more vulnerable.

Of the feral predators in Australia, cats are considered to be the most widely established. They are now found almost everywhere, in arid and semi-arid regions, alpine forests, woodlands and close to and within towns and suburbs. Most feral cats originate from unwanted pet cats being dumped in the bush. The offspring of the one-time pet become larger, wilder and tougher than domesticated cats and are fierce predators of wildlife. They have the ability to climb trees, gaining access to the native tree-dwellers' habitat.

Feral cats are fierce predators of wildlife. They can climb trees to gain access to bird nests, possums and gliders.

Effective control of feral animals is extremely difficult and enormously expensive for organisations responsible for managing land, such as the State wildlife authorities. Pet owners can help minimise the feral invasion by never abandoning unwanted pets. Unwanted pets can be taken to the RSPCA where attempts will be made to find new homes for them.

Domestic animal control

Pets also create problems for native wildlife. Although most owners of dogs and cats consider them harmless, they're not! Thousands of wild animals are killed or injured by pet cats and dogs every year.

Pet owners have a responsibility for the actions of their pets. All pets should be de-sexed as early as possible to prevent unwanted litters. Dogs should be kept under control at all times, either within a perimeter fence or accompanied by their owners. The movements of cats are much harder to control but cat owners can train their cat to come home before dark. If the cat is always fed at the same time each day—at dusk—then it will be motivated to come home at that time. Wildlife can be alerted to a cat's presence if the cat wears a few small bells on its collar. Foil wrapped around the cat's collar will also help wildlife notice the cat.

Both cats and dogs should be kept indoors at night. Most Australian mammals are nocturnal, that is, they are active at night, and if cats and dogs are allowed to roam during darkness, native animals can easily fall prey to them. By allowing pets to be out only during the day, the nocturnal animals will be safer when they go about their activities at night.

Ideally, domestic cats should be maintained in a 'cat-run', which gives them an enclosed area of the garden but prevents them from hunting native wildlife. Releasing unwanted cats and dogs in the bush is not only very cruel to the animal concerned but can be devastating to the native animal population. If the abandoned animal survives the ordeal, it will kill a multitude of native animals to sustain itself and may breed, producing more feral predators.

The pest control problem: some alternatives

Many chemicals are now commonplace around the home. The dangers associated with the use of chemicals, however, is not fully understood. The direct and indirect effects on wildlife and the environment may be harmful and totally undesirable. Some snail baits can also be fatal to birds and blue-tongue lizards if they eat the poisoned snails. This can then result in more snails because their natural predators have been killed. Wherever possible, biological control or harmless non-chemical alternatives should be sought instead of using substances for which the ecological consequences are unclear. We know little about the possible long-term effects of many chemicals on the environment. But we do know that there are some

Cat with bell.

Insect control can be assisted by providing nesting sites for birds, as many bird species feed their young on insects.

concerns, for example, about the use of rodenticides, which have affected the barn owl in urban areas. There are some well-known cases, such as the North American Peregrine Falcon, which suffered significant reduction in numbers due to pesticide use. Before applying any form of pest control, it is worthwhile considering the need for doing it.

Biological control may be a far more suitable option. Insects in the garden are part of the food chain. If they are destroyed, the chances are that a number of insect-eating birds will also be disadvantaged by the reduction in their food supply. Even worse, if the insects are treated with poison, the birds could also be poisoned after feeding on the insects.

In many cases, if active pest control is necessary, an alternative to chemical control can be found.

One of the easiest ways to combat pests is to encourage their natural predators, such as birds, frogs, spiders or lizards. It may take some time before the natural balance is restored once the reliance on chemicals is broken. Eventually, by encouraging the pest's natural enemies in the environment, the pest control job will mostly be done by your local wildlife. Alternatively, non-toxic substances can be used.

The following pages contain some suggestions for alternative pest control and recipes for pesticides and repellents.

Do you know what a monotreme is?

Echidnas and Platypuses are called monotremes because they reproduce in a different way from both placental mammals and marsupials. Both the Platypus and the echidna lay eggs. This egg is laid into the pouch on the female's belly. After the young hatches, it sucks its mother's milk, not from a nipple but from mammary glands on her belly.

Ant control

Ants can be useful in the garden as they eat some other insect pests and may even attack termite mounds. If ants become a problem, they can be controlled by spraying the nest with one part eucalyptus oil diluted with 10 parts water. Ant baits can be bought at chemists and supermarkets (Ded-ant or Antrid) and placed in an empty container with holes in the lid. Position the container in the path of the ants so that they can move in and out through the holes—the lid will prevent the bait being eaten by birds or other non-target animals. Ant mounds in paved areas can be treated with methylated spirits. Pour half a litre into the hole followed by half a litre of boiling water.

Planting herbs like tansy or pennyroyal near doors, and scattering the dried leaves of these herbs on shelves and window ledges, will stop the ants from coming into the house.

Prevention Ant infestations can be prevented by removing food sources and improving hygiene. For example, seal cracks and crevices in the kitchen, wash dishes after use, wrap up rubbish before putting it in the garbage bin and store food in airtight containers, wash dog and cat bowls immediately after use and remove the sugar bowl from the kitchen table.

Cockroach control

Baits can be made by putting lard in an empty margarine container. The cockroaches will go in but can't get out because of the slippery sides. Glue traps can be bought in supermarkets and work effectively for cockroach control. Vaseline placed on cardboard and sprinkled with crushed cat biscuits will also trap cockroaches. Bay leaves and cucumber peel kept moist are also effective in controlling cockroaches.

Prevention Increase hygiene; for example, wipe down benches, wash dishes after use and wrap up rubbish before putting it in the garbage bin. Reduce breeding areas, that is, fill cracks and crevices, particularly in warm areas such as behind the hot-water system. Store food in airtight containers.

Moth and silverfish control

To kill an infestation of moths or silverfish, place clothes in black plastic bags in the sun for a few hours. Dried lavender in cloth bags scattered among clothing will keep fabric pests away, as will eucalyptus oil in a small container with air holes.

Prevention Regularly air clothing outside and avoid putting stained or soiled clothing in drawers or wardrobes.

Fly control

Flyswats can be used to kill flies and sticky flypaper can be hung in places where flies congregate, such as in kitchens.

Prevention Increase hygiene, particularly in the kitchen, and be sure to wrap up garbage in newspaper before putting it in the garbage bin. Flyscreens can be installed on all windows and doors. Eliminate breeding areas for flies by removing cat and dog faeces from the direct home environment, cleaning the kitty-litter tray regularly and covering the compost heap.

Fruit and vegetable pest control

A garlic and soap spray can be made from the recipe on page 11. This will deter many garden pests. Hand picking grubs and snails off plants takes time but is very effective. Alternatively some grubs can be hosed off with a garden hose set to produce a fine spray, or vacuumed off (for sturdy trees only).

Prevention Encourage natural insect enemies, such as insect-eating birds, to the garden. Establish plant combinations such as marigolds among vegetables and flowers to repel beetles; onions to repel aphids; and basil to keep diseases and pests from tomatoes. There are many books on herbs and gardening available that provide guidelines on plant combinations or companion planting. Ask your local plant nursery for some suitable options.

Mould and mildew control

Scrubbing with water and soap is still an effective way to eliminate mould.

Prevention Increase airflow through the house and fix any plumbing leakages —be sure to check this under the house, too. Ventilation under floors may need to be improved.

Funnel-web spider control

Pour boiling water, kerosene or mineral turpentine into burrows (wear protective shoes while doing this).

Prevention Eliminate dark, moist areas in the backyard and prevent entry to the house by having slippery strips of metal or gloss paint at access points, such as on the vertical section of steps. In areas prone to funnel-web spiders, wear heavy gloves, shoes and socks when gardening and never leave clothes or shoes on the ground outside. If gardening shoes and gloves are kept in a garden shed, shake them out vigorously before putting them on.

Garden insect control (mites, scales, aphids)

Try any of the following mixtures to deter these insects: buttermilk and flour spray; soap and garlic mix; or glue mixture. Recipes are listed on the next page. Companion planting with marigolds may also help control aphids.

Prevention Encourage natural insect enemies, such as insect-eating birds, to the garden by providing them with suitable habitat (see Chapter 2).

Mosquito control

Personal herbal insect repellent and fly-swats can be used—herbal repellents are available from health food stores and chemists.

Prevention Install flyscreens and erect a mosquito net over the bed. Breeding areas, such as still water in old garbage bins, old paint cans, buckets and pots, should be eliminated. Native fish; for example, small surface-swimming Rainbow Fish, can be introduced to garden ponds to keep mosquito larvae down.

Rodent control

Traps and baits must be laid in such a way that possums and gliders will not be affected. Traps and baits can be placed under a wire basket without a base. Rodents will burrow underneath to reach the food while possums and birds will not burrow and, therefore, will not be able to reach the trap or bait. Remember, however, that a half-dead mouse is an easy catch for a bird of prey. Most poisons used for rodents will also affect birds. Try to use prevention and traps in preference to bait.

Prevention Rodent-proofing the house can be carried out by a pest control company. Increasing hygiene, particularly with more regular sweeping and vacuuming in food preparation areas, will reduce the food available to rodents. Covering the compost heap or composting in a bin with a lid will also help to control rodents.

Snail control

Non-chemical snail baits can be made by placing milk or beer in an empty plastic margarine container. This is then set in the ground, level with the soil. The snail can get into the container but not out.

Sawdust or ash from a fireplace will make barriers if sprinkled around the vegetable garden but must be renewed after rain. Snails can be hand-picked off plants at night when the snails are more active and can easily be found with a torch. Terracotta plant pots placed upside down on a stick in a moist part of the garden make a great daytime shelter for snails and slugs. The snails can be collected from these each day and destroyed. Permanent barriers can be made by putting 10 cm high galvanised fences around precious young plants or entire vegetable gardens.

Prevention Encourage lizards and birds into your garden to control snails.

Homemade pesticides and repellents

Buttermilk and flour spray

$^1/_2$ cup buttermilk
4 cups wheat flour
20 litres water

Mix well and use in a spray gun. (Kills mites by suffocation.)

Garlic and soap spray

$^1/_2$ cake of soap
1 teaspoon crushed garlic
5 litres of hot water

Mix well and let stand for 24 hours. Spray as a repellent for sucking and chewing insects. Dilute with 5 more litres of water if used on non-woody plants.

Glue mixture

100g fish glue or other animal glue
5 litres warm water

Mix well and spray trees and bushes to trap and kill aphids and scale insects. (The glue flakes off when drying, trapping the insects and removing them from the tree.)

Food
AND SHELTER

P ossibly the greatest threat to Australian animals is the destruction of suitable habitats. We can help local native animals by preserving and creating suitable habitats in our backyards, local parks and reserves. If residents and councils cooperate with each other to create wildlife corridors, substantial increases in animal habitats can be achieved, thereby increasing their chances of survival. Many species are struggling and many are in decline as they try to sustain themselves in a much-changed world. Some admirable initiatives have been implemented around the country but much more can be done. All of us have a role to play. We can begin in our own backyards and lead by example.

Which animals are around?

As a first step in creating a suitable wildlife habitat, it is a good idea to investigate which native animals you are going to attract and cater for. Start by visiting a local area containing native vegetation. The best times to visit such areas are early morning, late afternoon and at night—

Do you know what we call animals when there is more than one?

- a colony of ants
- a swarm of bees
- a brood of chickens
- a school of dolphins
- a flight of doves
- a charm of finches
- a school of fish
- an army of frogs
- a flock of galahs
- a gaggle of geese
- a siege of herons
- a smack of jellyfish
- a mob of kangaroos
- a colony of penguins
- a bevy of quail
- an unkindness of ravens

the times when many animals are most active. Observing and noting the animals you see will give an indication of the ones likely to visit your garden. Remember to look in the treetops, in bushes and on the ground. When you visit the area at night, use a strong spotlight (about 100W) to locate nocturnal animals that may use the area, such as possums, gliders, bats, bandicoots and owls.

For additional information, contact the local office of the wildlife authority, such as the National Parks and Wildlife Service or the State equivalent, which may be able to provide you with a list of animals present in nearby national parks.

Armed with this information you can attempt to re-create a suitable habitat for the most common species. Basic requirements for some common urban wildlife are listed over the next few pages.

Which plants do the animals use?

When planning your garden, it is important to remember that different animals use different plants and different layers of vegetation. If we consider three main layers of vegetation:

◆ animals most commonly using the top layer, which might have tall eucalypts and angophoras, would include possums and gliders, ravens (crows), kookaburras, currawongs, magpies, Black-faced Cuckoo-shrikes, fruit bats, Dollarbirds, cockatoos and lorikeets.

◆ the middle layer of dense shrubs and small trees may include banksias, grevilleas, tea-trees, and mock-orange and is commonly used by possums and gliders, finches, wrens, robins, spinebills and honeyeaters.

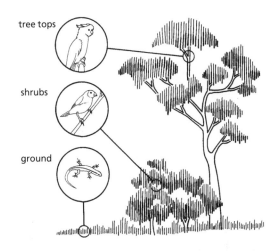

The three main layers of woodland vegetation:
1. the top layer is tall trees which provide the canopy; **2.** the middle layer consists of shrubs and bushes; **3.** the ground layer is comprised of grasses, herbs and leaf litter.

◆ the bottom layer, consisting of grasses, vines, ground-hugging or dwarf species of banksias, grevilleas and other ground covers, is used by small ground skinks, blue-tongue lizards and shingleback skinks for shelter and protection, as well as bandicoots, native rodents, dasyurids (small carnivorous mammals), finches, wrens, pardalotes, echidnas and quails.

This is by no means a comprehensive list, merely an indication of possible users. The types of animals present differ from habitat to habitat and from State to State due to differences in local environments. A list is given on page 25 of the types of vegetation that can be grown in an average suburban garden to provide food and shelter for native animals.

Common wildlife and their basic needs

Echidnas

Natural habitat: wide variety of ground habitats that supply ants and termites.
Food: ants and termites.
Shelter: under thick bushes, in hollow logs or occasionally a burrow; often use soil and leaf litter to conceal themselves.

Bandicoots

Natural habitat: from rainforest to dry woodland.
Food: insects, fruits and soft tubers.
Shelter: shallow hole in the ground lined with grass and leaves or occasionally a burrow; often uses soft soil and leaf litter to conceal itself.

Blue-tongue lizards

Natural habitat: areas with ground cover.
Food: insects, snails, native fruits and flowers.
Shelter: hollow log, under leaf litter or rock shelter.

Wrens

Natural habitat: shrubby vegetation.
Food: variety of small insects.
Nesting: in dense bush; nest is small dome shape made of grasses, lined with wool and feathers.

Honeyeaters

Natural habitat: areas with flowering trees and plants.
Food: nectar and insects.
Nesting: cup-shaped nest in a shrub or low tree; nest is made of plant fibres, grasses and spider webs, generally suspended by its rim.

Finch

Natural habitat: variety of habitats near native grasses.
Food: native grass seeds.
Nesting: nest made of grasses, usually built in thick bush; nest usually domed with a funnel entrance.

Seed-eating doves and pigeons

Natural habitat: lightly wooded grasslands.
Food: seeds.
Nesting: stick-nest in fork of tree or thick bush.

Swallows

Natural habitat: woodland and open country.
Food: flying insects.
Nesting: nest is a cup of mud and plant material, often built on the side of a tree or building; some species nest in tunnels in river or creek banks.

Possums

Natural habitat: forest and woodland areas.
Food: eucalypt leaves and flowers, fruits and buds of native vegetation; frequently forage for household scraps.
Shelter: tree-hollows; ringtail possum also builds nest, called a 'drey', in dense shrubs.

Gliders

Natural habitat: tall, open forests and woodland.

The Blue-faced Honeyeater has a varied diet. It feeds on nectar, pollen, fruits and insets.

Food: acacia gum (wattle), eucalypt leaves and sap, manna and insects (the greater glider eats only eucalypt leaves).
Shelter: tree-hollows.

Flying foxes (fruit bats)

Natural habitat: large trees in forests or mangroves, for roosting.
Food: variety of blossoms, nectar and fruits of native trees and orchard trees.
Shelter: roosts in large trees with adequate foliage to give protection from the weather.

Cockatoos and rosellas

Natural habitat: prefer tall trees for roosting.
Food: variety of native and exotic seeds and fruits.
Nesting: tree-hollows.

Brushtail possums have adapted well to living near people and are common in most urban areas.

15

Lorikeets

Natural habitat: timbered areas.
Food: pollen, nectar, blossoms, fruit, seeds and insects.
Nesting: hollow limb of a tree.

Kookaburras

Natural habitat: woodlands and open forests.
Food: snakes, lizards, nesting birds, frogs, rodents and insects.
Nesting: hole in a tree.

Magpies

Natural habitat: woodland with tall trees.
Food: insects, worms, slugs, frogs and carrion.
Nesting: stick-nest high in tree, lined with wool, hair and grass.

Creating a habitat

By growing a wildlife-friendly garden with suitable habitat plants, it is possible to extend animal ranges to areas where they have not been able to survive for years. But the success of a wildlife garden depends on careful planning and preparation. Before establishing such a garden a number of points need careful consideration.

Although native plants are preferable, not everyone will want an entirely native garden. Established exotic trees can be integrated successfully with native plants. Although exotic trees tend not to produce the nest hollows that eucalypts do, they can provide other essentials for wildlife. For example, the liquidambar, cotoneaster, hawthorn and mulberry provide plentiful food and shelter for native birds and other animals. However, the use of non-native trees or shrubs that have a tendancy to invade native bushland should be avoided. Examples of these are privet, camphor laurel, wild tobacco, blackberry and lantana. The seeds are eaten by birds and the birds' droppings help the spread of these plants.

In the initial planning of the garden, a general study of the site should be undertaken. Take note of the wind direction, the position of the sun and shade throughout the day in both winter and summer, the location of existing trees

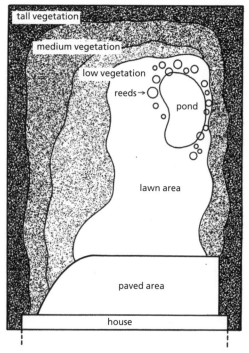

Drawing the garden on paper first allows for creative designing and inspired gardening.

and plants, buildings and overhead wires, and the type of soil. The local climate also needs to be considered: find out the amount of rain, the degree of humidity and the number of frosts you have in your area as well as which parts of the garden remain wet after rain.

Once the site has been analysed, it is helpful to draw a map of the area to be planted. On graph paper, mark the existing trees and other vegetation that you wish to retain. Also indicate areas with good drainage as well as wet areas. This will help you to select plants for those conditions.

Next, consider where you want sun and shade in the garden. You may want the verandah, deck or a barbecue area to be shaded from the midday sun in summer but sunny in winter. This can be achieved by careful selection of species and choosing the right spot for them, remembering that the sun is higher in the sky at midday in summer than it is in winter. Some Australian trees are deciduous, losing their leaves in winter. An example is the flame tree (*Brachychiton* spp.), which can be used to provide shade in summer and allow for sun in winter.

This is also the time to decide how much of the garden will be lawn. A garden with large areas of lawn will attract fewer animals—and different animals from one with less 'open' space.

During the planning process you may also wish to consider the use of vegetation to increase privacy around your home.

The types of plants to be used should be based on your plan along with other factors, such as flowering times, the particular needs of each plant (amount of water, sun or shade, type of soil and so on), size when fully grown, animals that may benefit from them, whether they are fast-growing or slow-growing species and the life span of each plant. Use a book on native plants or walk around a nursery before deciding what to plant.

When planning the selection of plant species, consider the layers of vegetation as discussed on page 13. If the taller species are planted around the perimeter and the smaller ones in front, this will make the garden look bigger. It also allows a better view of birds in the middle and bottom layers of vegetation.

It is also important to consider all the types of food you could grow, such as fruit, blossom, nectar, juicy leaf tips and seeds. These food sources should be present all year. It is possible to plant types of trees and bushes that flower at different times of the year so there will always be some blossom and nectar to eat. Similarly, when planning the fruiting trees and bushes, try to have enough different species to cover the longest possible fruiting season in your climate.

Before planting, the garden may need some preparation, such as turning the soil. In some areas, compost or river sand should be added to the soil. Drainage could need improvement and some areas may need to be raised to achieve this. Logs and rocks can be used to retain the soil and at the same time will provide hiding places for lizards. Mounds are also suitable sites for plants that like good drainage.

Growing plants native to the area

There are direct benefits in planting vegetation that is native to your district. First, the local vegetation has evolved with the local climate and soils, so it is best suited to that particular environment. Second, the vegetation has evolved along with the local species of animals—each has adapted to the other over a long period of time. Their coexistence is mutually beneficial.

Local nurseries specialising in native flora will be able to advise on a selection of plants suited to your area's climate, soil and conditions. It might also be possible to collect seed or take cuttings for propagation from an established garden near you.

Collecting seed

Seed is often available from commercial suppliers or can be collected locally. However, seed from protected plants may not be collected, and nor is collecting allowed in national parks and nature reserves.

Not all seed is easy to germinate. It is a good idea to start with seed from species that have proved to be reliable, such as bottlebrush, eucalypt, hakea, wattle and casuarina.

The seed should be collected from a tree or shrub that is in a type of environment similar to the one where you want to grow your tree. For example, if the parent tree is located in a well-drained area, that is the type of area where you should plant the seedling.

Seed should be collected when it is mature—when the seed capsule looks brown and hard. The seeds should be placed on a tray and sun-dried each day. The seed capsule will eventually open to release the seed, which can be stored in sealed jars until planting time.

Germinating the seed

Some seed has a natural dormancy that can be broken by pouring boiling water over it. This includes all the seeds of the pea family, acacias and cassias. After a few hours of soaking, the seeds that have swollen are ready for germinating. Those that have not swollen can be soaked again.

Tubs, punnets, small pots or trays can be used for planting. It is not necessary to buy new ones—recycled yoghurt or margarine pots with holes in the bottom are ideal.

Many commercial potting mixtures retain too much water for Australian native plants which generally like well-drained soil. A good potting mix for the seed can be made up of 80 per cent river sand and 20 per cent peatmoss. The mix should be moist but not wet and should be spread to a depth of approximately five centimetres in the container. Scatter the seeds over the mix, about one

Recycled yoghurt or margarine containers make excellent pots for seedlings.

centimetre apart, and then cover them with another light layer of sand and peat-moss mix. The seed tray or punnets should then be placed in a warm spot, but away from direct sunlight.

The seedbed should be kept moist but watering must be done carefully to avoid damaging the small seedlings—a fine spray is best.

Transplanting

Once a seedling has grown two pairs of leaves, it is large enough to transplant to an individual pot. Put some potting mixture in a pot, make a hole in the potting mixture with a stick and place the seedling gently into this hole. Take care not to damage delicate taproots at this stage. Press the soil gently around the seedling. Continue caring for the seedling by providing it with diffused sunlight and enough water to keep the soil moist.

Planting in the garden

Planting is best done in autumn to give the new plant time to harden before winter. It is also easier to keep plants sufficiently watered in pots during summer. Before planting, soak the pot in water then allow it to drain thoroughly.

Seedling with two pairs of leaves.

Dig a hole in the ground—slightly larger than the pot—and fill it with water. Gently remove the young plant from the pot. When all the water has drained from the hole, the plant can be put into it. The soil that was taken from the hole should be put back firmly around the plant and watered again. The soil level around the plant should be about half a centimetre below the surrounding ground level to prevent run-off.

At this point, mulch can be added to the garden. Mulch of leaf litter, compost and twigs has a number of advantages: it provides food for the plant, reduces weed growth, retains soil moisture, provides hiding places for animals, such as lizards and bandicoots, and gives the garden a natural look.

To retard weed growth effectively, the mulch can be laid over a layer of newspaper (six sheets) and must be at least 10 cm deep. Take care not to put the mulch too close to the stems of the plant as this can cause 'collar-rot' in some species.

Cuttings

Many Australian trees and shrubs can be reproduced from cuttings. (Eucalypts and some acacias are an exception but they can be grown from seeds.) An advantage of this method is that the new plant will be an exact reproduction of its parent. In other words, if an individual tree or shrub flowers abundantly or grows very dense, the cutting will also have these qualities—provided, of course, that it is grown in similar climatic and soil conditions.

When a cutting is taken from a large-leaved plant, the leaves should be reduced in size to reduce water loss through evaporation.

Cuttings should be taken from new growth—between December and March is a good time. The cut should be made just under a node, the point from which the leaf grows, and the cutting should be about 5–10 cm long. Once the cutting is taken from the plant, it can be kept moist in a plastic bag in the refrigerator until it is ready for potting. Cuttings can be stored this way for up to a week but results are better if planting is done within a few hours.

The bottom half of the cutting will be placed into soil so the leaves from that end need to be cut off. Large-leafed plants should have all remaining leaves cut to half their size. This will reduce water loss through evaporation.

A good potting mix for cuttings can be made up by mixing two parts of river sand, with one part of peatmoss. Place this mixture in any type of container, but one that is at least 10 cm deep with drainage holes.

The cutting should be placed in a hole in the potting mix and the soil pressed gently around the cutting. Several cuttings can go in the same pot. They should be kept in a warm spot with diffused sunlight and must be watered regularly.

Usually roots will develop after one to three months, but some species take longer. The cuttings are ready to transplant to larger individual pots once the roots start showing through the drainage holes.

To transplant cuttings, the roots need to be carefully separated and the cuttings placed in individual pots by holding the cutting in position and filling the pot around it. Planting out should be done in the same way as seedlings.

Maintenance

It is preferable to give the young plants a good watering once a week rather than a little each day. By watering once a week, the roots are encouraged to go deeper to find water and thus stronger roots will develop.

Weeds must be kept away from the young plant for at least a year as they will compete with the young plant for nutrients and water and can retard its growth.

Is it okay to feed wildlife?

The feeding of wildlife, although it is enjoyable, is not recommended. In fact, it should be avoided. Providing food in the form of native plants is the preferred way of feeding as this is a natural supply of food. Native plants also provide essential requirements, such as shelter, safety and nesting sites. (Suitable food plants for wildlife are listed on page 25.)

Artificial feeding can have a damaging effect on an animal's health and may

At sunrise, flocks of Rainbow Lorikeets can be heard in many urban areas as they fly noisily to feeding areas.

alter its natural behaviour. Usually the food we can provide for wild animals does not have the nutritional balance found in the wild. This may result in serious health problems for the animals, such as obesity, nutritional deficiency diseases, reduced breeding success and viral and bacterial infections.

A dramatic example is provided by rainbow lorikeets, which readily feed on food put out for them by people. This food is often a mixture of bread, sugar and water or a honey and water mix which, unfortunately, the birds prefer to their natural food. But this artificial diet is deficient in protein and many vitamins and minerals. The Rainbow Lorikeet's natural diet is very high in protein and includes pollen, nectar, berries, seeds and insects. The protein, for example, is needed for growing new feathers once a year after moulting but, as there is very little protein in sugar and honey, birds that are fed this diet lack the protein to make new feathers. Every year hundreds of Rainbow Lorikeets are found with feathers too short for successful flight and, sadly, the birds that cannot fly usually fall prey to cats and dogs as they can't get away. Inadequate nutrition may lead to a compromising of the animal's immune system, making it more susceptible to disease.

The potential to spread disease is another concern related to artificial feeding. Rainbow Lorikeets eating from the same dish are prone to pick up all kinds of illnesses from each other. The food dish put out for the birds as a well-meaning gesture can become a source of contamination as one sick bird may infect all others that come and feed that day.

Feeding wild animals can also change their behaviour. Most animals occupy their time finding food. If the food is presented to them 'on a plate' and regularly, there is little else for them to do. This may seriously affect an individual animal's behaviour and change the social behaviour of animals living in groups.

If you do choose to feed wildlife artificially, the diet you provide must be balanced. Emergency diets for adult wildlife are discussed in Chapters 5, 6 and 7 and are suitable as supplementary diets to the natural diet. Ensure that the food is fresh and food dishes are cleaned thoroughly each day.

Safety from humans, pets and feral animals must also be ensured when food is provided for wildlife. Offer food on cat-proof feeding platforms or next to a cat-proof tree.

It is preferable to attract wildlife into your backyard by way of habitat creation or retention—the provision of the basic needs of life. There is more to life than food! Many animals will be attracted by a

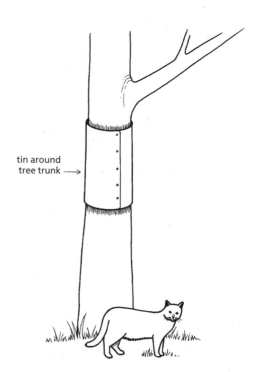

tin around tree trunk →

Trees can be made cat-proof by nailing tin around the trunk to prevent cats from climbing.

pond, a birdbath, safety from predators or suitable shelter and nesting sites. Take pleasure in seeing the wildlife feeding safely in the trees and bushes that you have planted and feasting on the insects around them.

They all need to drink

A good alternative to feeding wildlife may be providing water. A supply of fresh, clean water is beneficial to most animals and will also create more activity in the garden. Water can be provided in the form of a birdbath or a pond.

Birdbath

Birds will use a birdbath for drinking and bathing. When bathing, birds are often less aware of possible danger around them. The splashing of their wings could attract the attention of cats nearby and it is therefore important to locate the birdbath next to, or under, a cat-proof tree (see page 22) so that an escape route is close. For the birds' safety, the bath should be at least one metre off the ground. The higher the bath is placed, the safer it will be for the birds. It is essential to clean out birdbaths daily as a dirty bath could pass on disease from one bird to another.

A simple birdbath can be made using the lid of a metal garbage can for the 'bath' and a clay drainage pipe inserted into the ground for the pedestal. Attach a brick to the lid handle with wire and hang the brick down the pipe. The weight of the brick will keep the bath stable, and the design allows for easy

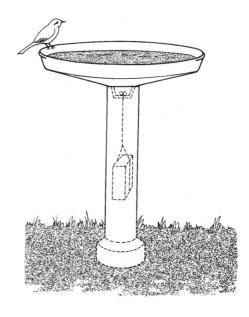

A simple birdbath, as described below.

cleaning. The metal lid can be painted to blend in with the surroundings, but always use lead-free paint around animals. Many nurseries and garden shops have a range of birdbaths for sale.

Ponds

An artificial pond adds an interesting feature to the garden and, more importantly, it creates additional habitat for wildlife. It is likely that frogs will eventually colonise the pond but you can speed up this process by releasing some tadpoles or spawn from a friend's or neighbour's pond.

The pond could be placed in an already damp part of the garden. This would allow you to grow reeds and other 'wet' vegetation, such as native rushes, ferns and irises, around it. To make the area suitable for frogs, shade should be provided over at least half the pond's surface. Shade is best provided by planting bushes and reeds around the pond. Avoid locating the pond under tall trees as fallen leaves will tend to clog it up. It is also essential to avoid a location under poisonous trees, such as oleander or pines, as fallen leaves may contaminate the pond water.

The pond is also best located where run-off from rain does not flow into it. Run-off may also bring fertilisers and pesticides from neighbouring properties.

Moulded fibreglass ponds are available commercially but they have disadvantages in that the size and shape are predetermined and many are very shallow. Planning and building your own pond gives you greater flexibility to determine its shape and size.

An attractive bush pond can be built economically using the following guidelines:

1 Excavate the site to the size and shape you want with shallow edges and a depth of between 50 cm and 1 m in the centre. The shallow edges will allow animals to drink from it and birds may bathe in it too.

2 Smooth the excavation site as much as possible and line it with UV-resistant, heavy-duty PVC sheeting or non-toxic pond liners. (Some liners may be coated or impregnated with chemicals.) Take care not to puncture the sheeting. Lay it loosely to allow for some movement and leave a wide overlap.

3 Surround the pond with bush rock, bricks, railway sleepers or logs to stabilise the edges. Some logs, rocks and branches can be placed half in and half out of the water to create a transition zone between water and land.

4 Place a layer of soil on the pond liner approximately 10 cm deep. Fill the pond with either rainwater or tapwater but add a few buckets of water from a local pond or creek. This will introduce micro-organisms to the pond which will help to establish a 'pond environment'. The water must be allowed to settle for at least two weeks before any planting is done.

5 Plants for garden ponds are available from many nurseries and a specialist native nursery will give advice on local wetland species. Plants floating on the surface of the water can include species such as *Nymphoides* spp. (marshworts) and *Ottelia o ali-folia* (swamp lily). Plants suitable for the submerged pond edge can include *Eleocharis sphacelata* (tall spike rush), *Typha orientalis* (cumbungi) and *Marsilea* spp. which are ferns. Plants can be placed in pots or directly in the soil. It may be beneficial in the long term to plant most pond vegetation in pots as it will be easier to control rapid growth.

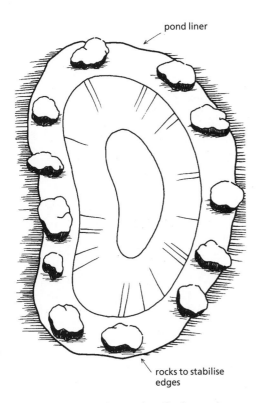

pond liner

rocks to stabilise edges

Pond construction, as described opposite.

Food plants for birds

Acacia spp., wattle
Acmena smithii, Lilly Pilly
Allocasuarina spp., she-oak
Arctotheca calendula, capeweed
Atriplex spp., saltbush
Calandrinia spp., purslane
Callistemon spp., bottlebrush
Callitris spp., native pine
Carex spp., sedge
Carthamus lanatus, saffron thistle
Casuarina spp., she-oak
Ceratophyllum demersum, fox tail
Chenopodium spp., goosefoot

Cirsium vulgare, spear thistle
Cleome viscosa, tickweed
Cucumis myriocarpus, prickly paddy melon
Dactyloctenium radulans, button grass
Danthonia spp., wallaby grass
Digitaria spp., umbrella grass
Eucalyptus spp., eucalypt
Echinochloa spp., barnyard grass
Eleocharis spp., spike rush
Eleocharis dulcis, bulkuru sedge
Ficus spp., figs
Fimbristylis spp., fringe rush
Grevillea spp., grevillea
Hakea spp., needle bush
Juncus spp., rush
Lepidium spp., peppercress
Maireana spp., bluebush
Marsilea spp., common nardoo
Melaleuca spp., tea-tree
Morus spp., mulberry
Paspalum spp., paspalum
Poa spp., tussock grass
Polygonum spp., smartweed
Potamogeton spp., pond weed
Romulea rosea, Guildford grass
Rumex spp., dock
Schinus areira, pepper tree
Scirpus spp., club rush
Scirpus litoralis, coastal club rush
Scleria spp., razor grass
Setaria spp., pigeon grass
Stellaria spp., chickweed
Stipa spp., spear grass
Trichodesma zeylanicum, cattle bush
Trifolium spp., clover
Triodia spp., spinifex
Typha orientalis, cumbungi
Vallisneria spiralis, ribbon weed
Xanthorrhoea spp., grasstree

Shelter and nesting sites

As the lack of suitable habitat is one of the main problems faced by urban wildlife, planting a variety of appropriate plants will provide a wide range of wildlife with shelter from predators and create sites for nesting. In addition, artificial nest-boxes can be used by mammals and birds in places where natural nesting sites are not available.

Tree dwellers

A wide variety of plants is used by tree-dwelling birds and mammals for nesting and roosting. Ringtail possums, for example, often build their nests from sticks and leaves in tea-trees or paperbarks, whereas brushtail possums use tree hollows. The western pygmy possum also uses tree hollows but sometimes builds its nest in the leaves of a grasstree (*Xanthorrhoea* spp.). Birds such as parrots and kookaburras also use tree hollows, whereas magpies and currawongs build stick-nests in the forks of trees.

Trees and bushes that provide adequate shelter and nesting sites for birds and other animals are numerous and some examples are listed on pages 32–34.

Many small species of birds, such as spinebills and finches, will use bushes with prickly foliage for protection. These include *Hakea sericea*, needle bush, and *H. teretifolia*, dagger hakea. Good nesting sites for smaller birds are also found in *Acacia armata*, kangaroo thorn; *A. boormanii*, Snowy River wattle; and *A. echinula*, hedgehog wattle. Medium-

The Common Ringtail Possum is a rather sociable animal—up to eight individuals have been observed sharing the same nest.

sized birds, such as wattlebirds, butcher birds and magpie larks, often nest in *Callitris rhomboidea*, Port Jackson pine, and *Casuarina cunninghamiana*, river oak, using the branches of the tree to support their nest. Larger birds, such as

Magpies build their stick nests in the forks of tall trees.

cockatoos, kookaburras and magpies, usually use taller trees for roosting and nesting, for example, eucalypts (gums) and angophoras, which closely resemble them. Magpies and currawongs make stick-nests in the treetops whereas cockatoos, kookaburras, lorikeets and rosellas use the hollow limbs of old trees.

Possums and gliders sometimes use the hollow limbs of large old trees during the day for shelter. Many Australian trees do not form nest holes until they are more than 100 years old. This is why it is important to preserve large, old 'habitat' trees.

Artificial nest-boxes

In the urban environment, hollow limbs tend to be removed from park and garden trees. Dead trees, which also provide valuable nesting sites, are usually chopped down as they may be of danger to

A suitable nesting hole in a tree trunk or branch may be used year after year to house the young of resident kookaburras.

A branch or a rope that links from tree to tree can be used to give possums access to a neighbouring tree. It would be unlikely for a cat to use this.

humans. The absence or removal of these hollow limbs and dead trees forces their users to look for residence elsewhere.

Artificial nest-boxes have been used with great success for many years, particularly in Europe and the United States of America. They allow species to re-establish themselves in urban areas where, for a long time, they have been unable to live successfully. In Australia, artificial hollows or nest-boxes have been used for Sugar Gliders, Feathertail Gliders, Brush-tailed Phascogales, brushtail possums, ringtail possums, Greater Gliders, King Parrots, pardalotes, Crimson Rosellas, Eastern Rosellas, galahs and many more native animals.

Nest-boxes should be placed in trees that have been cat-proofed. This can be done by nailing a wide strip of tin sheeting around the trunk of the tree (see page 22). Cats are unable to climb past

this. However, if the nest-box is for a mammal such as a possum, the tin sheet might also prevent the possum from getting up or down the tree. To provide access for the possum, a branch or rope can be attached to a neighbouring tree. Cats would be unlikely to use this.

Nest-boxes are sometimes invaded by wasps and bees, which must be cleared out as no animal will share a house with these insects. A beekeeper might be able to assist with this task.

Second-hand or new timber can be used to construct nest-boxes but bear in mind that some woods are more durable than others. Nest-boxes made of copper chromium-arsenic treated radiata pine will require little maintenance and the arsenic in the timber will not affect the animal. If the boxes are to be painted, make sure the paint is lead-free as some animals will chew the entrance hole and lead paint will poison them.

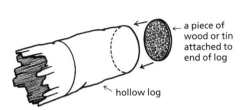

a piece of
wood or tin
attached to
end of log

← hollow log

Hollow logs, closed at one end, are used by a variety of mammals, such as possums and gliders, for sleeping. Birds such as kookaburras and parrots will also nest in these logs.

eaves

← edge board to
prevent chicks
falling from
nest

Platform for a swallow nest under the eaves of a house.

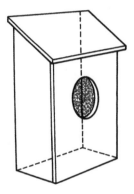

Nest-box for tree-dwelling mammals.

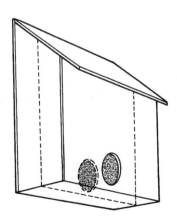

Roosting box for insectivorous bats.

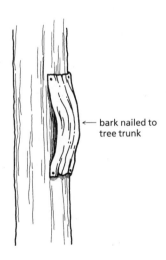

← bark nailed to
tree trunk

Bark nailed to a tree trunk with galvanised nails gives shelter to treecreepers.

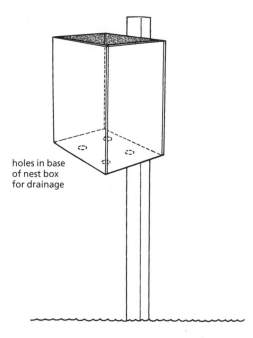

holes in base
of nest box
for drainage

Nest-box for waterfowl, placed approximately
1.5 metres above the water level.

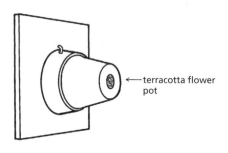

←terracotta flower
pot

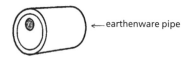

←earthenware pipe

Flowerpots and earthenware pipes provide
nesting sites for little birds, such as thornbills.

Did you know that the Platypus' bill, apart from its shape, is not like a duck's bill at all?

Unlike a duck's bill, the Platypus' bill is soft, pliable and very sensitive. When hunting for food under water, the Platypus closes its eyes, ears and nostrils. Most of the information it receives about its surroundings underwater comes from electronic receptors on the skin of the bill.

Ground dwellers

It is also important to provide shelter for ground-dwelling mammals, birds and reptiles, such as bandicoots, native rodents, quail and lizards. Ground cover, in the form of ferns, dense, low bushes and clumps of native grasses, is essential. Examples are *Themeda australis*, kangaroo grass; *Poa* spp., tussock grass; *Sorghum leiocladum*, wild sorghum; and *Danthonia richardsonii*, wallaby grass. Further shelter can be provided by hollow logs on the ground and clay drainage pipes under bushes. The gaps in rockeries also provide ideal shelter for native rodents and lizards. Lizards will readily use rockeries for safe basking in the sun as hiding places can be quickly accessed in the event of danger. Try to provide some flat rock basking areas that catch the first sun of the day. If a safe hiding place is nearby, lizards will love to come out early in the morning to warm up their bodies.

Welcome swallows often return to the same nest or a site nearby year after year.

Providing natural nesting materials

Other materials used by animals for nest construction can be provided in the garden. Many birds use the 'down' from the cones of *Banksia serrata*, saw banksia, for nest lining while others use the papery bark of *Leptospermum laevigatum,* coastal tea-tree. Birds use spiders' webs in their nest construction and, for this reason, many people may decide not to remove webs around the exterior of the house during spring and summer. Some birds, such as swallows, use wet mud to build their nests, which are often constructed on ledges under the eaves of houses, in outhouses or in garden sheds.

Native grasses grown in clumps provide nesting material for birds and mammals, as well as food for native rodents and seed-eating birds, such as finches. Bandicoots and native rodents, for example, often line their nests with these grasses. Native grasses look attractive in the garden and do not need mowing.

There are many other different and favourite nesting materials and some of these can be hung in the garden for the birds to select. Short strings of natural wool or cotton, unspun wool or cotton and small tufts of kapok can be loosely gathered and hung in a net—the type of net in which you buy oranges or onions is perfect for this purpose.

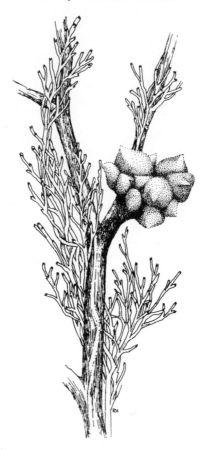

Callitris rhomboidea (Port Jackson pine)

Shelter trees for birds

Following is a list of plants that have the characteristics that are preferred by animals for shelter and nesting. If the plants listed are not native to your local area, an equivalent can be found. A native nursery should be able to assist.

Shelter trees

Acacia baileyana, Cootamundra wattle
A. decurrens, early black wattle
Callistemon viminalis, weeping bottle brush
Callitris rhomboidea, Port Jackson pine
Castanospermum australe, black bean or Moreton Bay chestnut
Eucalyptus camaldulensis, river red gum
E. sideroxylon, pink-flowered ironbark or mugga
Grevillea arenaria, Nepean spider flower
G. aspleniifolia (no common name)
G. speciosa, red spider flower
G. robusta, silky oak or silver oak
G. shiressi, Mullet Creek grevillea
Hakea leucoptera, silver needlewood
H. nitida, shining hakea
H. propinqua, blacknose
H. salicifolia, willow hakea

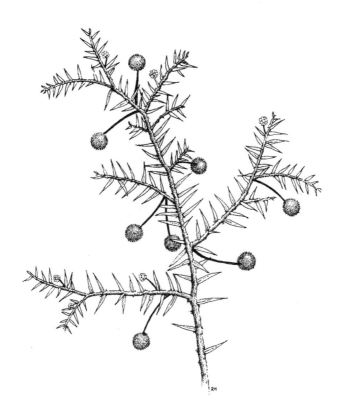

Acacia ulicifolia (prickly moses)

Kunzea ambigua, white kunzea or tick bush
Leptospermum flavescens, yellow tea-tree
L. juniperinum, prickly tea-tree
L. laevigatum, coastal tea-tree
Melaleuca armillaris, giant honey myrtle
   or bracelet honey myrtle
M. quinquenervia, broad-leaved paper
   bark
M. styphelioides, prickly paperbark
M. wilsonii, violet honey myrtle
   or Wilson's honey myrtle
Persoonia levis, broad-leaf geebung
Pittosporum undulatum, sweet pittosporum
Syzygium luehmannii, onionwood

Native plants for nesting birds

Acacia armata, kangaroo thorn
A. boormanii, Snowy River wattle
A. ulicifolia, prickly moses
Banksia serrata, saw banksia
Bursaria spinosa, sweet bursaria
Callistemon citrinus, Crimson bottle
   brush
Callitris rhomboidea, Port Jackson pine
   or Oyster Bay pine
Casuarina cunninghamiana, river oak
Clematis aristata, traveller's joy or old
   man's beard
Dryandra guercifolia, oak-leaf dryandra

Callistemon citrinus (crimson bottlebrush)

D. sessilis, holly-leaf dryandra
Eucalyptus calophylla, marri or white
    flowering gum
E. capitellata, brown stringybark
E. camaldulensis, river red gum
E. melliodora, yellow box
E. microtheca, coolibah
E. rossii, inland scribbly gum
Gleichenia dicarpa, pouched coral fern
Grevillea rosmarinifolia, rosemary
    grevillea
Hakea petiolaris, sea-urchin hakea
H. propinqua, blacknose
H. sericea, needle bush or silky hakea
Leptospermum juniperinum,
    prickly tea-tree
L. laevigatum, coastal tea-tree
Melaleuca decussata, cross-leaf honey myrtle
M. wilsonii, violet honey myrtle
Pandanus spiralis, screw palm
Rhagodia spinescens, hedge saltbush
Toona australis, red cedar

Placement of nest-boxes and roosts

For most species of wildlife, it is beneficial to place the nest-box at least three to four metres above the ground. Protecting the animal from attacks by predators is of paramount importance.

Grevillea rosmarinifolia (rosemary grevillea)

Boxes should be placed on the trunk or major branch of a tree and not in a fork. If it is put in a fork, the nest-box may be crushed as the tree grows. The entrance should be positioned to face away from prevailing wind and rain. Nest-boxes can be attached to the trunk by fitting leather, plastic or metal strips to the nest-box and nailing these to the tree with long, galvanised nails.

Nest-boxes for mammals must be placed in a tree with branches that interlock with those of other trees. This reduces the need for the animal to walk on the ground where there is danger from predators and cars. If this can't be done, use a cut branch or a rope to link nearby trees to the tree with the nest-box. Attach ropes about three to four metres above the ground where possible.

Roosts for insectivorous bats can be placed either under the eaves of a house or in a tree approximately three metres above the ground.

For birds such as small parrots, cockatoos and kookaburras, the nest-box needs to be placed five to six metres above the ground. For swallows, the roost can be placed at approximately three metres above the ground, for example,

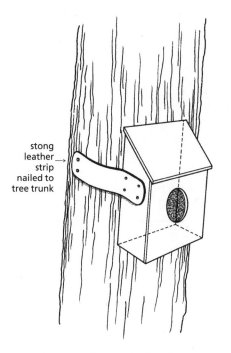

stong leather strip nailed to tree trunk

under the eaves of the house. Waterfowl boxes can be placed at about one-and-a-half metres above the water surface.

To allow rainwater to run off, all nest-boxes must have sloping roofs or be attached at a sloping angle.

Ringtail possums in the wild make nests from branches and twigs. Instead of a nest-box, they can be given an artificial nest. These can be made by attaching two wire hanging-plant baskets (including liners) to each other to form a sphere. Make a small entrance hole for the possum in the fibre liner. Hang the nest high in a dense tree such as a tea-tree or an old banksia. By attaching a rope to the nest and throwing this over a branch, the nest can be placed high in a tree.

Nest-boxes can be attached to the tree trunk with leather, plastic or metal strips. These can be nailed to the tree with long galvanised nails.

Guide to the dimensions of nest-boxes			
Species	Minimum height above ground	Diameter of entrance	Depth below entrance
Brushtail possum	4 m	10–12 cm	28–30 cm
Ringtail possum	4 m	6–8 cm	25–40 cm
Feathertail Glider	2 m	3–5 cm	10–40 cm
Sugar Glider	4 m	3–6 cm	20–45 cm
Insectivorous bats	4 m	3–5 cm	0 cm
Eastern Rosella	5 m	7–10 cm	35–80 cm
Galah	6 m	12–14 cm	60–70 cm
Lorikeet	5 m	5–7 cm	60–70 cm
Kookaburra	5 m	12–14 cm	level
Waterfowl	1.5 m	10–12 cm	45–75 cm
Barn Owl	5 m	platform only	platform only
Swallow	3 m	platform only	platform only

1. *Warm and cosy*. A woollen beanie helps this young Greater Glider feel secure.

2. *No returns*. Dainty Green Tree Frogs are often found in boxes of bananas. To prevent the spread of a fungal disease, they cannot be returned to their place of origin.

3. *Sweet rewards*. Banksias provide a good source of nectar for a variety of animals including honeyeaters, bats, other small mammals and insects.

4. *Long-term commitment*. A furless wombat may need special care for some ten to twelve months before it can fend for itself in the bush.

5. *Thin and oily*. This oiled Little Penguin is very thin. The oil destroys the waterproofing of the feathers and hampers normal fishing. Even a partially oiled bird can loose a lot of weight in just a few days.

6. *Dehydration can kill*. Birds affected by oil pollution such as this Little Grebe are usually very dehydrated. Before handling or cleaning, these birds should be tube fed with a warm rehydrating solution.

7. *Bird bath*. This magpie was covered in oil when it fell into sewerage sludge. It was given several baths in warm soapy water to remove the oil. The soap was then rinsed out of the feathers with a warm shower.

8. *Marsupial nest builders*. Ringtail possums build nests called dreys. They often use branches of tea trees and paperbark trees lined with shredded bark and grass.

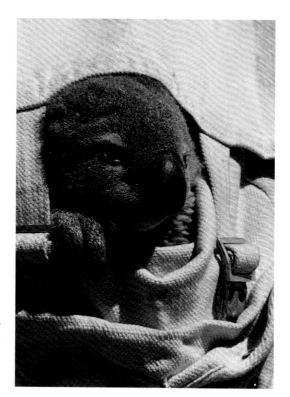

9. *Backpacker*. This Koala is fully furred and does not need artificial heat. It is comfortably transported in a backpack with a woollen pouch and a cotton liner.

10. *High perches*. Tree-climbing snakes such as this Diamond Python will appreciate a climbing structure within their temporary enclosure.

11. *Ouch!* Echidnas have effective and simple protection.

12. *Soft underbelly*. An echidna's belly is the only place without spines. Rolled up in a ball its belly is protected.

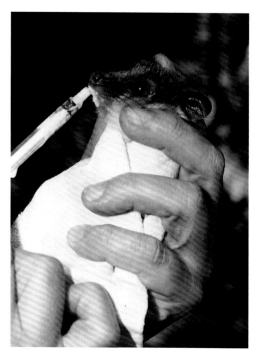

13. *All wrapped up*. Orphaned possums are often reluctant to drink initially. For the first few feeds it may be necessary to wrap them up to stop them struggling. They soon learn to lap from the end of a syringe.

14. *Sponge baths*. Young bottle-fed animals need to be cleaned after each feed. Over time, any milk left under the chin or food on the fur can cause skin infections.

15. *Lapping it up*. Once the juvenile animal starts to feed on solid foods it can soon be taught to lap milk. Initially the animal is gently held over the milk bowl until it laps voluntarily.

16. *All alone*. Young ringtail possums and other social possums and gliders fret if they are not kept with others of their species. They are best looked after in little groups of similar-aged animals.

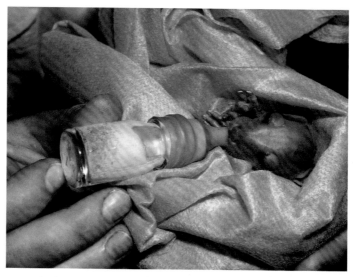

17. *Naked possum—keep warm*. Furless marsupial youngsters such as this Brushtail Possum get cold quickly. They have to be wrapped up and cosy, even during feeding.

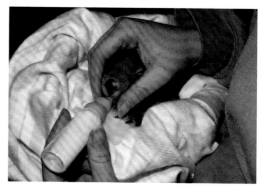

19. *Blinkered*. Newly orphaned animals are often difficult to feed. By covering this wombat's eyes and ears it is less distracted and likely to feed better.

18. *Out of his tree*. This young Sugar Glider fell to the ground when the tree in which it lived was lopped. After its recovery from mild concussion, it was released with a nest box in which to shelter.

20. *Wild Koalas bite and scratch.* Koalas can be safely caught when in an enclosure. By pushing on its head it can be made to walk backwards into a hessian sack.

21. *As good as new.* This Crested Hawk broke a leg in a collision with a car. Before release it is given whole carcasses to make sure it can use its healed leg well.

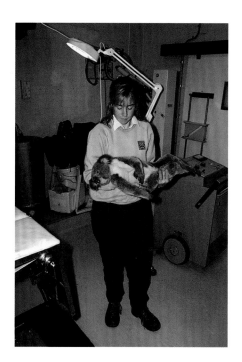

22. *Knock out.* This Koala was hit by a car while crossing a road. A vet has sedated the animal so it can be X-rayed and checked for broken bones. All car accident victims should be checked for fractures.

23. *Weight watcher.* This young Palm Cockatoo is being weighed regularly during hand rearing to make sure it is putting on the right amount of weight.

24. *Found alive*. Always check the pouch of female kangaroo road victims. Often live young, such as this Bridled Nailtail-wallaby, are found relatively unharmed in the pouch.

25. *Lethal danger*. A ringtail possum killed by a fox. Foxes, feral and domestic cats and dogs are a serious threat to native wildlife.

26. *Born to be wild*. Hand-reared juvenile animals such as this Eastern Grey Kangaroo need to learn to be 'wild' before they can be released. They are best kept in a predator-proof paddock with other kangaroos for some time before release.

27. *Comfy seat*. Cage furniture for Koalas should always include a comfortable perch to sit on. They can be housed temporarily in an aviary as long as it is dog proof.

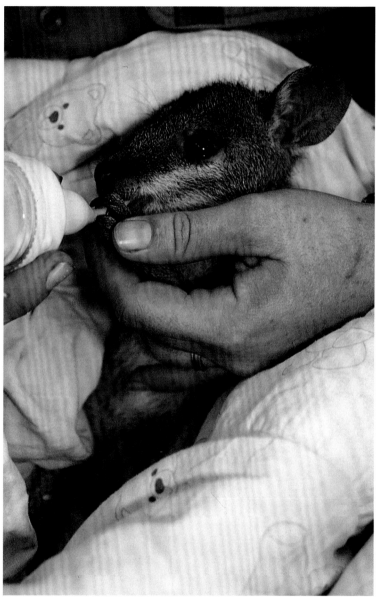

28. *No cow's milk please*. Marsupial young such as this Spectacled Hare-wallaby are intolerant to the lactose in cow's milk. Marsupials must always be fed a special marsupial milk formula.

29. *Basket case*. This young currawong fell out of its nest on a windy day. The nest was too high to reach. The bird was given a basket lined with cloth and tissue paper as an artificial nest and put back in the tree. Its parents continued to care for it.

30. *When enough is enough*. Young birds such as these Welcome Swallows will beg for food when they are hungry. To avoid over-feeding they are only fed when they 'gape' (beg with open mouth) vigorously.

31. *Dangerous when handled*. Goannas can inflict serious bite wounds. Always use thick leather gloves. Quickly grasp the animal around the shoulder area while securing the back legs at the same time.

32. *Soaking it up*. Many sick, injured or traumatised animals become dehydrated, including snakes. This Diamond Python is given a rehydration solution under the skin to restore its normal fluid balance.

33. *Tiny sips for tiny lips*. This young insectivorous bat is fed a milk formula from a syringe. These small bats are not often rescued when sick or injured. Only weighing a few grams, they are probably overlooked when on the ground.

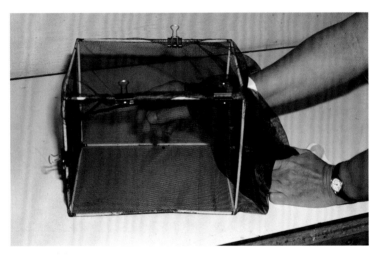

34. *Safety net*. Insectivorous bats can be housed safely in a wire frame covered with light-weight fly-screen netting. Cover the enclosure with a towel for privacy.

Case Studies:
ENCOUNTERS WITH WILDLIFE

This chapter discusses some specific but fairly common examples of encounters with wildlife.

Kangaroos and cars

One of the most common reasons for kangaroos and wallabies coming into captivity is car accidents. Run-off of water from roads makes the grasses next to them grow thick and juicy. Kangaroos often feed on these, making them vulnerable to vehicles travelling by.

Alway check the pouches of dead marsupials by the side of the road as live pouch young may be present. After checking for pouch young, move the carcass off the road so it does not attract other wildlife, such as birds of prey, to the same fate. Make sure you do not place yourself in danger when rescuing an animal. Some wildlife groups spray a paint signal on the carcass so others know the animal has been checked for live pouch young.

If a female kangaroo is killed but her joey is found unharmed or relatively uninjured inside the pouch, you can give it a good chance of survival by taking the following steps. Furless joeys are difficult to remove from their mother's teat as their mouth will have closed very firmly around it. To remove the joey from the teat, hold its head from behind in such way that your thumb and forefinger are at the 'hinges' of the jaw. Apply gentle pressure on either side of the mouth until the joey releases the teat and it can be slid out without too much resistance. Do not pull as the joey's mouth can be damaged in this process. If the teat will not come out easily it may be cut off. Attach a safety pin and a piece of cloth to the teat so there is no chance of it being swallowed by the joey after it is cut off. The joey will release the teat more easily later, once there is no more milk being produced.

The young animal may have been in its dead mother's pouch for hours or even days. Cold and dehydration are probably its main problems (see page 103). An emergency kit can be carried in the car so that injured animals on the road can be helped. This kit could include:

- disposable gloves—wear when checking pouches and removing carcasses off the road
- torch—useful during night-time rescues
- blanket, woolsack, towels—these can all be used to capture and restrain a distressed animal
- pillowslips and wool pouches—to put joeys in after rescue
- hotwater bottle—to provide warmth for cold animals
- feeding utensils—bottle, teat and rehydration solution (see page 103)
- scissors—to cut the teat if a joey can't be removed otherwise
- cardboard boxes—useful for transporting small animals.

Transport an injured animal to a veterinarian as soon as possible for examination. Local wildlife authority representatives, such as rangers, will be able to give advice on the availability of local veterinarians.

Animals crossing the road

Animals need to move between areas—for their food resources, to find water or to search for a mate. For these reasons animals often find themselves on a road. Some animals are in no hurry to cross and are very vulnerable to accidents. You may wish to help such animals move to a safer place. Some of the more common situations are listed here, with some guidance on what to do. However, you must first weigh up the personal dangers and never risk your own safety.

Echidnas An echidna may stop in the middle of the road if startled by traffic. If it stays there it will almost certainly be run over. Echidnas are difficult to pick up but if you use a thick towel doubled over or a similar thick cloth, it is unlikely you will get hurt. Put the towel over the echidna and pick it up around the centre of its body. Let the animal go after you have walked some distance beyond the edge of the road, about 20 or 30 metres. Be sure to take the animal in the direction it was facing, otherwise it may soon head back onto the road.

Snakes Snakes are often seen sunning themselves on the tarmac of the road. Tarmac warms up quickly in the morning and heats the snake from below, while the sun warms it from above. Some Australian snakes are venomous and they can strike at you from the full distance of their own body length—so keep your distance and stay in your car. There is little evidence that snakes respond well to airborne sounds. If a snake needs to be scared away from an area, it is better to use vibration as a warning signal. Do this by driving the car near the animal in the hope that it will notice the vibrations and move off the road. Alternatively you could use a long stick to touch the rear end of the snake while you remain in the car.

Turtles Turtles that need to cross the road often 'freeze' when they're in the middle. If a car passes and frightens them as they are crossing, they will pull in their head and legs as their normal defence mechanism. They stay in this defence position for some time and are obviously very vulnerable. Turtles can scratch with the claws on their feet and spray a pungent, foul-smelling secretion from their musk glands when they are alarmed. The exact function of this is not known but it is thought to be a defence mechanism. Pick up the turtle carefully with two hands around the body, keeping your fingers away from the mouth. Hold the turtle at arm's length so that your clothes are not stained with the secretions. Walk to the edge of the road in the direction the animal was facing. If you can see water nearby, release the turtle in water. If there is no water, release the animal some 20 to 30 metres from the road. If you happen to know that there is no water available in the direction in which the animal was going, put the turtle in a cardboard box and take it to the nearest body of water.

Ducks   Ducks and ducklings crossing the road can cause some concern. Some people get out of their cars and try shooing the animals along. There is a risk of separating the animals by doing this and it is better simply to stop the car (or the traffic) and give the parent ducks time to move their brood safely to the other side.

Birds   Birds of prey feeding on a carcass on the road run the risk of being run over themselves. If it is possible without endangering yourself, move the carcass off the road using disposable gloves or a shovel. Once the carcass is off the road, the birds of prey will be a lot safer.

Most other animals on the road are just moving through and all they need is time to get away from speeding vehicles. Take care on country roads and particularly around dusk, dawn and during the night, when many animals are most active.

Possum in the roof

Lying awake and listening to what sounds like a football game on your roof is not the most pleasant way to pass the night. If a possum has found access to your roof and is enjoying a romp, oblivious to your need to sleep, the most reasonable solution, in terms of the possum's livelihood and your sanity, is to find a compromise by providing the possum with a home in your yard. First, you can try to discourage the possum by making the roof environment as unpleasant as possible. Strong lights can be set up in

Do you know the 'his and her' names for animal species?

Species	Female	Male
bird (general)	hen	rooster/cock
cattle	cow	bull
duck	hen	drake
fox	vixen	dog
geese	goose	gander
goat	nanny	billy
(general)	dam	sire
horse	mare	stallion
kangaroo	doe	buck
seal	cow	bull
sheep	ewe	ram
swan	pen	cob
whale	cow	bull

the roof, and strong smells, such as cloves and garlic, will deter possums. This method is not always successful. The preferred solution is to trap the possum (see below, for guidance on building a trap) and keep it in the trap in a warm, dark and quiet place while you block off any entrance holes to the roof. As well as blocking off holes, lop off any branches that overhang the roof to remove the access points. Check the roof carefully for other possums, as ringtail possums live in small groups.

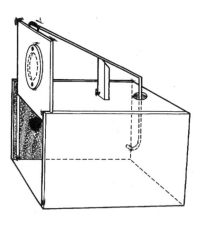

A possum trap which can be converted into a nest-box by removing the round entrance cover.

Do you know what to do about raiding possums?

To prevent possums from raiding your vegetable garden, build a corrugated iron fence around the vegetable garden that is about waist-high. Make sure that there are no trees overhanging the fence. Possums can't climb this fence.

Once you have taken measures to prevent the possum re-entering the roof, prepare a new home for it. Select a strong branch in a tall tree and attach the trap, which now becomes a nest-box for the possum. Do not remove the entrance cover until just before dark. For easy viewing of the possum you can attach a feeding platform to the tree and place some titbits on it, such as banana, apple or other fruit. The possum now has somewhere safe to live and cannot get back into your roof.

The above procedure is preferable to the more common practice of renting a possum trap. If you trap the animal and release it a long way from home, it will be released into another possum's territory where its survival chances may not be good. In an unfamiliar environment, the possum would have to search for shelter and may be unable to avoid danger. It is abandonment verging on cruelty. If for some reason the blocking off of access to your roof is impractical or impossible, and relocation of the possum seems to be the only option, permission from the State wildlife authority must be obtained prior to trapping.

Animal in the house

A possum in the roof is not the only visitor you might encounter. Occasionally, other wildlife can end up in the house. The first step, if you have pets, is to lock the cat and dog away so they can't damage the animal or be damaged themselves. Some common situations are described below with some suggestions on how to deal with them. If you feel unable to deal with the situation yourself, contact the State wildlife authority for advice or for referral to a local wildlife rescue group.

Possum in the house The animal usually enters through an open door or window. Its normal reaction, once it is inside, is to panic, and this can create quite a mess. It is not uncommon for people to arrive home and think their house has been burgled, with decorations scattered and vases and ornaments knocked over. If you are home when a possum has entered, you probably want it out—and fast.

First, try opening all the doors wide, switch off the light so the animal may feel less alarmed and gently herd it towards the door. If that fails to work, it is probably best to switch tactics. Secure all valuable ornaments and confine the possum to one room. Think about the layout of the room it is in and how this is going to help you corner the animal and catch it. Holding a thick towel or blanket, move slowly and confidently towards the possum and herd it into a position where you can catch it more easily. Throw the blanket over it and quickly gather all corners firmly around it. Roll any loose flaps of material around the animal and take it outside. Assuming it is still night, release the possum under a tree by loosening the material around it and letting the animal come out of the bundle of its own accord. The possum could be disoriented as a result of its recent experience. Switch off outside lights and move away so that the animal can regain its composure.

Bird in the house Birds often fly in through open windows and find their way out again. Occasionally a bird will panic once inside and start to crash into closed windows, mistaking the glass for the way out. First, close all curtains so the bird will not injure itself by flying into the glass. Then open all the doors wide while gently herding the bird towards the nearest opening. Don't chase the bird but move calmly around it. If the bird is in a real panic and starts to fly into solid objects, leave the room with all the curtains closed and doors open and allow it to settle. The bird may find its way out once it calms down. If the bird still does not leave of its own accord, try herding it again for a couple of minutes. If there is still no success, there are a couple of alternatives. The bird can be netted with a butterfly-type net or wait until nightfall. Allow the room to remain in darkness for an hour or so then switch on the lights and try to catch it. Sleepy birds are very easy to catch. Make the bird comfortable in a cardboard box or cage until the next morning. Release the bird at first light.

Snake in the house Venomous snakes should only be handled by experienced herpetologists. If you are unsure of the species of the snake, do not attempt to handle it. Contact the State wildlife authority for advice or referral to a local wildlife rescue group. Observe the animal to see where it goes and keep an eye on it from a safe distance. Keep children well away from the snake. Block access to the rest of the house by closing as many doors as possible, except the doors through which it could exit. Allow the animal some time to get out voluntarily. You could help it along by creating a lot of vibration—this tends to alarm the animal and it may decide to leave. If it does not leave, call for assistance and wait. There are now many wildlife groups and zoos that will send a reptile handler to remove reptiles in dangerous situations. Someone will come and assist you.

Do you know why some birds tap on the window?

During the breeding season there are many reports of birds 'tapping' on the window. The most common reason is that the bird sees its reflection in the window and thinks an intruder has come into its territory. Each time it taps on the window it is attacking the 'intruder'.

Lizard in the house Lizards wander into houses regularly. Usually no action is required as the animal is not dangerous. There are no venomous lizards in Australia. It is a myth that blue-tongue lizards are venomous—this is entirely untrue. So do not worry about the lizard and it will move away again as it is unlikely to find much to eat inside your house. If you really want the lizard

removed, gently guide it in the right direction with a soft broom. Do not touch the animal—just encourage it to move in the required direction.

Flying fox in the fruit tree

Flying foxes feed on pollen and fruit and in doing so they disperse the seed of native trees and shrubs. They also play a role in pollinating native trees. However, damage to fruit trees is also attributed to these mammals. It appears that flying foxes prefer and need their indigenous foods of native figs and eucalypt flowers. Damage to exotic fruit trees is usually greatest when the native trees fail to flower significantly.

Flying foxes are protected in all States of Australia. A licence is needed from the State authority to destroy or trap flying foxes that are causing damage to fruit trees. To protect your peach tree or other fruiting tree, the bats can be deterred in several ways. Most methods involve netting the tree or frightening the bats away using bright lights, noisy bells or tins dangling in trees. These are the most cost-efficient methods for urban residents growing non-commercial crops.

Flying foxes are drawn to the site by the smell of ripe fruit, so picking the fruit early will prevent damage to fruiting trees. Avoid leaving rotting fruit on or around the tree as this will also attract these bats.

No one method of preventing fruit damage by flying foxes seems to be totally successful. Further research into the behaviour of these bats is needed in order to find a solution for the

Flying foxes feed on pollen and fruit and in doing so they disperse the seed of native trees and shrubs.

orchardist. However, long-term solutions to this problem include planting more native vegetation and retaining local bushland so that the bats' natural food is more abundant.

Magpie parents

The magpie is a well-known feature of the Australian landscape. These birds live close to people and their carolling can be a source of delight. However, magpies lose their popularity during the breeding season, from August to October. This is when their urge to defend their territory becomes very strong and the instinct to expel intruders affects people who happen to live in the magpies' territory.

Magpies intimidate human intruders by flying low and clacking their beaks as they pass overhead. Very occasionally, a magpie might actually strike the intruder on the head. Birds showing this sort of aggressive behaviour may have been interfered with in the past. For example, they may have had a previous nest destroyed by humans and have consequently become more protective.

A simple way to avoid attack in the short term is to wear a hat or hold an umbrella. Better still, wear a plastic ice-cream container or hat with eyes drawn on the back—this helps to deter the magpies. In the long term, the birds can be befriended by occasionally feeding them. Suitable food for magpies is tinned dog food or dog kibble soaked in water. The birds will learn not to fear humans to the same extent and the magpie breeding season may be more pleasant for all concerned.

Destructive cockatoos

Some home owners have their fascia boards or railings chewed to pieces by cockatoos and an effective solution to this problem has not yet been found. Often the cockatoo offenders are being fed by someone in the neighbourhood and the birds are passing the time as they wait for breakfast or lunch. It is a good idea to ask around the neighbourhood and talk to anyone who is feeding these birds. People may be persuaded to give up the feeding if they understand that this might be the reason the birds are staying and causing damage in the area.

If the birds are perching on the roof or a railing, a trip-wire will make landing difficult. Being 'tripped' when landing may discourage them from landing there again. The birds can also be discouraged by noise, such as clashing pots and pans, or by spraying water with a high-pressure hose. Strips of foil that flutter in the wind can also be a deterrent. However, these

trip wire

Wire can be attached just above the bird's favoured landing place. This will 'trip' the bird when landing.

measures will also deter other birds from visiting your garden, including those that you may like to have around.

In the longer term, damage by cockatoos can be prevented by planting tall eucalypts. The cockatoos are more likely to chew the trees than your house, and you can then enjoy the other bird species around the garden without the destructive cockatoos attacking your home.

Unwelcome visitors to the garden

If the presence of certain animals in the garden worries you, the deterrents are the exact opposite of the suggestions for attracting them. To deter most wildlife, all that is required is a lack of suitable habitat for that species. If there is nowhere to live, nest or feed, the animal will not remain in your garden. Following are some specific suggestions that can be used to deter wildlife:

Snake in the garden   Not everyone likes to have snakes living in their garden, particularly when they are close to houses or children. A herpetologist (reptile expert) can identify the snake and, if necessary, remove it to a safer place, both for the sake of the animal and the people. The local wildlife authority will be able to recommend a herpetologist in your area. If the snake turns out to be a harmless species, you may decide to leave it where it is. Farmers often allow harmless pythons to live in their sheds to keep the numbers of rats and mice down.

Home owners can take some preventative steps to discourage snakes from encroaching too close to the house. These include cleaning up around and, in particular, under the house so that there are no hiding places, and fitting fly-screens to all openings. If the immediate home environment has no snake habitats, such as dark hiding places under the house or a sheet of tin to shelter under, the problem should not recur.

Goannas These creatures are particularly keen on gardens with an aviary or chicken coop. Make sure that aviaries are goanna-proof as they may burrow to gain access to the birds. Aviaries and chicken coops should be kept as tidy and odour-free as possible and should have a wire floor so that rodents and other predators can't gain access. Goannas may also be attracted to compost heaps, particularly if rotting meat is present. To discourage goannas, cover the compost heap daily or make compost in bins with lids.

Bandicoots These are magnificent creatures of which several common species have just managed to survive in urban and rural areas, despite significant predation by cats, dogs and foxes. Although much maligned for digging small holes in the garden, there is no evidence that the presence of bandicoots increases the likelihood of ticks in the garden. If you do wish to discourage this species from your garden, construct a bandicoot-proof fence around your property. Galvanised mesh with gaps no larger than 2 cm can be used. The mesh should be buried about 15 cm into the ground and should stand at least 50 cm above ground level. The presence of bandicoots is, however, an excellent way to control insects and spiders in the garden.

Penguins As penguins can be exceptionally noisy at night, particularly during the breeding season, they do not make good neighbours. People who live right next to the ocean can be kept awake by nesting penguins under the house singing their territorial songs. To keep the penguins away, it may be possible to block entrances to the area under the house with chicken wire or similar material. Be sure to do this in mid-winter so that there are no penguin chicks present that could be closed in. Penguins may also use the area for moulting. They get their new coat of feathers once a year and stay on land while the new feathers grow. This process is usually completed by April or May at the latest. If penguin-proofing is going to be carried out, June is probably a good month to do so. Alternative housing in the form of nest-boxes can be provided for penguins and should be placed in a sheltered position under dense vegetation, preferably not too far from the highest high-water mark.

Swallows Some types of swallows, such as Welcome and Barn Swallows, build nests under eaves or on the rafters of buildings. Some residents object to the amount of faecal matter that ends up on their verandah or patio. Relocation of nests is not usually successful so it is best to allow the parents to rear their clutch.

If you want to prevent them from nesting there again, some discouragement might be considered. Fine fishing line could be mounted about 10 centimetres from the wall on which they nested or near the rafters they used. Make sure the line is mounted in the birds' flight path. Use several strands of line and extend it the full length of the wall. As the birds come to investigate the potential nesting site, they will hit the 'invisible' wire and get a fright. Make sure the wire is taut and no loose threads are left dangling that the birds could tangle themselves in. This measure may not exclude the birds entirely but will certainly discourage them from re-using the site.

Birds in general Birds can be discouraged from the garden or certain parts of the garden by using a range of deterrents. However, if you manage to keep birds away from the vegetable patch, it is likely that you will also discourage the honeyeaters from the grevillea nearby.

The deterrents used most successfully with birds involve both sight and sound. Anything that flaps in the breeze will scare them off, such as empty wine cask bladders inflated and suspended, coloured and silver streamers, old-fashioned scarecrows and silhouettes of birds of prey in flight with outstretched wings.

Sound deterrents can include the occasional clanging of pots with a wooden spoon, tape recordings of a distress call from a bird or even a call from a bird of prey. The main trick is to move deterrents around regularly as the birds soon become used to them. By moving the offending objects or sounds around, the birds continue to be wary of them and may go elsewhere. Alternatively, use minor deterrents and provide a suitable diet for the birds in another spot in your garden. If they feed there, they may leave your home-grown food alone. Consider, however, the birds' value as insect controllers and plant a little more vegetation to feed them as a 'thank you' for their role.

Plover on the roof

Birds such as masked plovers nest on the ground. They scrape the soil and line the nest with grass and debris. In the urban environment they find the ground is often too busy and they choose flat roofs instead. The trouble starts when the young hatch. The parents usually roam widely with the flightless young in tow. The young birds don't fly for about six to seven weeks, after which they moult out of their downy coats and into their plumage with flight feathers. When their parents lead them to forage for worms and insects, the young birds fall off the roof. Many newly hatched plovers come into captivity with broken legs and head and internal injuries.

Some roofs are selected for nesting by plovers time and time again. The anxious home owner must look on in horror, knowing what will happen next—more injured baby plovers on the ground. It is possible to stop plovers nesting in unsuitable spots by scaring them away. In the case of nesting plovers, a cut-out silhouette of a large bird of prey with outstretched wings, as if in flight, will work well. The silhouette can be cut from plywood and should have a wing span of at least 60 to 80 cm. This can then be mounted on or near the roof so that it is silhouetted against the sky. Alternatively, a silhouette can be painted on a large balloon or on the roof itself. Old-fashioned straw scarecrows can also be used but must be placed directly onto the roof. As the animals will become used to the silhouette's or scarecrow's presence, the device should be moved regularly to another position.

Possums and roses

Some possums develop a taste for roses. Persistent individuals will come back night after night to munch on someone's precious blooms. There are several ways to discourage possums from eating the roses and it may be necessary to use a combination of methods. One suggestion is to use quassia chips. These are made from the roots of a South American tree and can be bought at some pharmacies. Some chips are boiled with water and allowed to cool, then strained (follow the instructions on the back of the packet). Discard the chips and spray the flowers with the quassia chip water. The spray is a deterrent only

and does not poison or damage the animals in any way. It simply makes the roses taste terrible and the possum will lose interest. The spray must be repeated after heavy dew or rain.

The spray will work equally well for possums that are raiding passionfruit vines or any other low fruit-bearing or flowering plant. It may be too much work to spray entire trees but this is likely to stop raiding possums in their tracks.

In addition, decoy food could be provided nearby to distract the animal from its mission. If the possum has to come to the ground to feed on the roses, it may be possible to deter it by spreading spiky or prickly material on the ground surrounding the roses. Use cuttings from prickly grevilleas and hakeas or rose stems with thorns.

> ### Did you know that pardalotes will often nest in a recently dug earth mound?
>
> These small birds dig a tunnel with a nest chamber at the end. When nesting in a mound in the garden this makes them very vulnerable to cat attack. Protect them by erecting chicken wire around the nest to keep predators away. This also gives the bird a safe entry and exit as only the bird itself is small enough to fit through the holes.

Entangled birds

Sadly, it is fairly common to see birds entangled in fishing line or caught by a fishing hook through the beak or body. These animals are difficult to help as they can often still fly and increase their injuries in their distress. By the time they come into care, the hook or line has often cut into the flesh so much that infection has started. The bird becomes weaker as its illness progresses. When it can barely fly it is caught more easily, but by then its condition may have deteriorated so much that the bird is difficult to save.

One way of catching these birds earlier is by feeding them for a few days and setting up a system. This will be different for each species.

Pelicans can be caught after feeding them for a few days by either grabbing the bill or approaching in a boat and lunging for the animal, grabbing its upper wings by the shoulder region. Then the bird can be transferred to a handler on the boat.

Silver Gulls and plovers can be encouraged to feed on the ground for a few days (but keep cats and dogs away). While 'free feeding' for a few days, have a trap in place. A trap can be made with wire mesh of any size, fashioned into a box shape. The trap should be five to ten times larger than the bird you want to trap. The door of the trap should also be mesh, slightly wider than the rest of the box. The door can be attached at the top only so that it swings down readily. The door is held open with an upright stick which has a length of rope attached to it.

Over a few days, feed the bird around the trap, then feed closer and closer to the trap. Start putting food inside the trap, without making any attempt to catch the bird. Once the bird starts to move in and out of the trap confidently,

the time is right to catch it. You may only get one chance to catch the bird—it will be a lot more wary if it has had a near miss. Sit quietly and keep yourself concealed while holding the end of the rope. When the bird is well inside the trap and feeding, pull the stick away and the trap should close.

Take the bird gently from the trap and carefully remove the fishing line or hook. If the skin has been broken and swelling or redness is present, the animal should be examined by a veterinarian and may require antibiotic treatment.

Lizards and whipper snippers

Lizards such as blue-tongues and Shinglebacks have managed to survive in many urban and rural backyards. Some of the more recent human 'toys', such as whipper snippers, cause these animals occasional harm. Many lizards are brought into care with deep lacerations due to contact with whipper snippers and lawnmowers.

First aid for these animals is essential as significant bleeding can occur. The animal should be bandaged to stop the bleeding. The bandage should be about as tight as you would bandage a sprained ankle. Make sure the animal can still breathe. Transport it to a veterinarian as soon as possible.

Some injuries can be prevented. For example, before you mow or use the whipper snipper, particularly in long grass, walk around the garden making noises and vibrating the ground by stamping your feet. The lizard should get the message that it is better to seek shelter for a while. This is especially important on cold days as the lizard may not have warmed up and will be slow to move out of the way of a cutting gadget.

By having lots of hiding places around the garden, you will make the environment safer for lizards. Sunning platforms that catch the early morning sun and have a safe hiding place nearby will mean the lizards are less vulnerable.

Wildlife and tree removal

When taking down large old trees, home owners are regularly surprised to discover evidence that the tree had been home to a range of animals. Examples of animals found regularly during tree lopping or removal are ringtail, brushtail and pygmy possums, Sugar and Feathertail Gliders, tree-dwelling snakes, insectivorous bats and many birds. Ask the tree loppers to examine any tree-hollows carefully before chopping the tree down. Animals may be removed and held until they can be released in a new nest-box or a section of renovated tree-hollow (see page 29). A section of hollow tree in which an animal lived could be given a new 'end' by sawing a smooth edge and attaching a wooden cover. Put the animal back in the nest-hollow and cover the entrance with a cloth taped firmly in place. This renovated nest-hollow could then be re-attached to a tree with the animal inside it. If more than one animal was found inside the same nest-hollow, they should all be put back together. Find a suitable tree nearby, or perhaps use the same tree if it was only lopped rather than felled, and attach the nest-hollow to a sturdy branch with rope or a strip of metal and galvanised nails. Try to find a position that is similar in terms of height and aspect to the original nest-hollow. For nocturnal animals, the taped cloth can be removed after nightfall. For diurnal animals, this can be removed once the animals have calmed down after the big move, say an hour or two after they were last handled. During the entire lopping operation, pets should be kept away from the area. Small birds may fall out of disturbed nests or mammals may fall with their nest-hollow. Cats or dogs are likely to get to the fallen animal before you do. It is possible to avoid bird casualties by taking into account that most birds nest in spring or summer. Any tree work done during autumn or winter is less likely to disadvantage birds in the short term.

When you have to remove a dangerous tree, consider replanting a native species that will benefit the wildlife.

Mound builders

Brush Turkeys build large mounds to incubate their eggs. The male Brush Turkey scratches available leaf mulch into a magnificent nesting mound about four metres wide and one to one-and-a-half metres high. The females of the species are attracted first to these mounds and, as a result, to the male. The female lays her eggs in a niche in the mound where fermentation of the rotting vegetable matter keeps the eggs at the correct incubation temperature. The male Brush Turkey scratches and turns the material and new mulch is added regularly for extra heat. This is a fascinating process—except when it takes place in someone's backyard in an inconvenient place.

The male may scratch material away in a radius of some 20 m around the mound. It is difficult to discourage a determined Brush Turkey but it is possible to redistribute the beginnings of a mound into the garden each night. The Brush Turkey may give up after some time. If not, you could get out the binoculars and watch this amazing display taking place in your own backyard.

A similar mound-building process takes place with mallee Fowl and Scrub Turkey. Mallee Fowl are unlikely to use domestic gardens but occasionally come close to human habitation. Both male and female Scrub Turkey build and maintain the mound. To discourage Scrub Fowl, daily redistribution of their scratchings may convince them to try elsewhere.

Lyrebirds also scratch earth together but the male lyrebird's mound is used for displays only. The male builds a mound of about 90 cm wide and 15 cm high. To attract a female, he performs a spectacular display on the mound, spreading his long tail in a fan and throwing it forward over his head. During the display, the male sings a medley of his own songs and the mimicked calls of other birds.

You can try to discourage these birds with the same tactics as for Brush Turkey and Scrub Fowl—but enjoying their presence and witnessing their behaviour is a lot more fun.

Birds in the roof

The common house sparrow was introduced into Australia in the nineteenth century to make migrants feel more at home by having familiar birds to look at. These birds do not build great nests, usually cramming their nests untidily in crevices of buildings, under eaves and bridges and in dense bushes and hollow limbs of trees. When sparrows nest in roof cavities or under eaves, the enormous amounts of nesting material are a potential fire hazard. In some cases the equivalent of two bales of hay may be removed from the eaves of one small wall. Occasionally chicks die in the nest or eggs fail to hatch, and the decaying material may smell. The best time to remove this material is outside the breeding season, otherwise you may need to make decisions about what to do with any chicks you find in the nest. The breeding season is generally in spring and summer but, if conditions are right, these birds can nest at any time. Remove all nesting material and seal all roof cavities and entry to eaves. Specially moulded foam in the shape of tin roof corrugations is available from hardware stores.

Emergencies
WHAT TO DO

S ometimes we are confronted with an injured native animal. The cat may have brought it in or it may have been found under a tree or by the roadside. By applying some basic emergency treatment you may be able to help save the animal's life.

Basic principles of first-aid for sick and injured native animals are similar to the first aid principles for domestic animals and people. The main differences are that the animal will be very frightened, it will try to defend itself and you will need to give special consideration to transporting, housing or feeding it. For most wild animals, any contact with humans is stressful. Normally a wild animal only comes into physical contact with another species as part of a predator/prey relationship. Efforts to comfort an injured wild animal in the way you might comfort an injured dog, such as by stroking it and talking to it, might be its death knell.

It is essential to take an injured animal to a veterinarian as soon as possible after any first-aid treatment. There may be internal injuries not visible to the untrained person. Meanwhile, the animal should be kept warm, quiet and in a dark place, such as a cardboard box.

In most States, a licence to hold native wildlife is required and your State wildlife authority must be contacted as soon as possible after acquiring the animal. Wildlife authorities for each State are listed in the reference section (pages 127–8).

General first-aid principles

Establish an airway

Ensure that the animal is able to breathe. Extreme care should be taken in holding and transporting the animal because this can easily restrict its breathing. Avoid holding the animal tightly around the neck or chest, tilting the head down or transporting it in a plastic bag. Unconscious animals should be placed in a position with the head above the level of the stomach to prevent choking. Remove any vomitus, blood or other matter from the mouth as the animal could choke on these

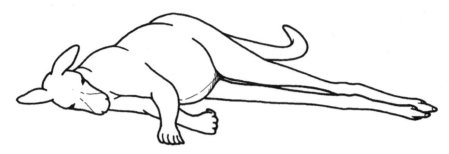

Unconscious animals should be placed in a position with the head slightly above the level of the stomach to prevent choking. The head and neck should be extended to ensure that the animal can breathe freely.

substances. The mouth or nose should be pointing downwards to allow any food or saliva to drain easily. The head and neck should also be extended to ensure that the animal can breathe freely.

Prevent major bleeding

External bleeding almost always looks worse than it is, but there may also be serious internal bleeding. Keep the animal quiet and as undisturbed as possible. This allows normal clotting mechanisms to take care of the problem and prevents aggravation of injuries by needless struggling. Unnecessary handling of a bleeding wild animal will stress the animal and temporarily raise the blood pressure, producing more bleeding. Major arterial bleeding is rarely encountered but, if present, this requires the application of a pressure bandage over the injury site.

Maintain body temperature

Body temperature is particularly important for smaller animals, for example,

rodents, orphaned joeys and birds. Most adult or large-bodied animals simply require protection from sun, wind and rain but, if these animals are injured or ill, artificial heating may also be needed.

For small animals, some form of indirect heat is best. Placing the animal inside your clothing is a good method of

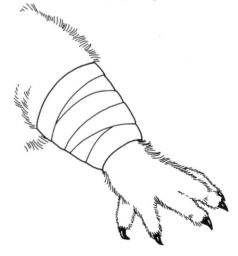

A pressure bandage can be used for major arterial bleeding. Ensure that the bandage is not too tight and does not restrict the animal's breathing.

warming for some of these animals. Electric blankets, heated waterbeds, pet warmers and electric frypans could also be used but take extreme care not to overheat the animal and always monitor the temperature closely. A well-wrapped hotwater bottle can be used in the short term but loses its heat quickly. Large variations in heat are a greater problem than constant low temperature. Much energy is needed for the animal to adjust its body temperature—energy it may not have.

In the case of most small animals, an external temperature of 32°C is sufficient to maintain body heat. However, tiny joeys and small birds are best kept at 35°C. The heat should preferably be provided in such a way that the animal can regulate its temperature by moving towards or away from the heat source. It is important to monitor the temperature closely with a thermometer or thermostat.

Treat for shock

The best first-aid treatment for shock is to keep the animal warm and undisturbed. In the longer term, medicated treatment for shock can be administered by the veterinarian. Never give alcohol or aspirin to wild animals.

Small mammals, such as insectivorous bats, feathertail gliders and very young orphaned joeys will benefit from the oral intake of high energy fluids. For emergency use, some Staminade or an oral rehydration solution for humans suffering from diarrhoea is probably sufficient. Offer it carefully, at body temperature, from an eye-dropper, syringe or similar device. Avoid force-feeding birds with an eye dropper, particularly with runny fluid, as the fluid often ends up in their lungs and may cause death. They can be offered the same solution from a dish. Carefully hold the dish up to touch the bird's bill. Do not cover the nostrils and do not force the bird to take it.

Minimise stress

Try to avoid causing stress as much as possible by keeping the animal quiet and undisturbed. Keep it away from the smells and sounds of potential predators, such as cats and dogs.

Most wild animals do not show visible signs of stress. Often the rescuer thinks the animal is 'settling down' when suddenly it dies. A very stressed mammal will often become quiet, giving the appearance of accepting its situation. Allow the animal to settle for 30 minutes or so before it is examined more thoroughly.

Common problems faced by wildlife

With each of the following problems the basic first-aid principles should be followed.

Automobile victims

Contact with vehicles is a common cause of injury to large mammals. Kangaroos, wombats, Koalas and the larger possums are frequent victims. Injuries may include head injuries, broken bones and internal damage, such as a ruptured bladder, liver and kidneys. First aid

Animals killed by cars and left on the road will attract meat-eating animals which, in turn, run the risk of being hit by a car.

should be given and the animal should be transported as soon as possible to a veterinarian for diagnosis.

Healthy, uninjured joeys are often found inside the pouch of a severely injured or dead female. Ensure that the pouch of a female marsupial is checked.

Prevention Drivers should be more aware that there may be kangaroos, wombats or other animals on the road, particularly at night, and slow down. Food should not be thrown from travelling cars as it may attract animals onto the road, thereby increasing their chances of being run over. Dead animals should be removed from the road. Animals killed by cars and left on the road will attract meat-eating animals, such as quolls (native cats) and Wedge-tailed Eagles, which also run the risk of being hit by a car.

Victims of predation

Birds, lizards and smaller mammals, such as rodents, small possums and insectivorous bats, often fall victim to the domestic cat. The victim should be carefully examined for tiny puncture wounds, since these may indicate further internal damage. Even small injuries caused by cat bites can lead to serious infections. All cat bites require veterinary treatment as infection is common. Unharmed animals can soon be released once they have recovered from shock.

Wounds caused by dogs are usually more visible. Larger animals are often bitten around the neck and chest and internal damage is common in these injuries. In most of these cases, veterinary examination and treatment is essential.

Prevention Do not feed native birds or tree-dwelling animals on the ground as this makes them more vulnerable to predation and disease. Several small bells attached to the collar of a domestic cat (see page 6) may alert other animals to the cat's presence. Pet owners should keep pets locked inside at night to reduce the threats to nocturnal native animals, such as gliders and bandicoots. Domestic pets should be de-sexed. Unwanted litters should never be disposed of in the bush because the animals will either grow up to be ferocious hunters or will die slowly of starvation.

Poisoned animals

Poisonings do happen from time to time but can be extremely difficult to diagnose. Usually poisoning is suspected when a number of animals are found in the same area showing similar signs of illness or weakness. There are many different types of poison that may show any of the following signs: vomiting, difficulty in breathing, frothing from the mouth or nose, fitting, diarrhoea, stumbling and lack of vision. The rescuer should not treat the animal other than with basic first aid and should transport the animal rapidly to a veterinary surgery.

Prevention When any chemicals are used, manufacturers' instructions and warnings should be strictly followed. Alternative non-chemical control methods for use around the home are outlined in Chapter 1 (page 11).

Bushfire victims

After severe bushfires, scores of animals may be found suffering from the effects of fire and smoke. The signs will vary but general first aid for fire victims is as follows:

- smoke damage to eyes—avoid touching the eyes and have the animal treated by a veterinarian. Meanwhile keep the animal out of bright light and away from heat or fumes
- respiratory problems due to smoke inhalation—transport to a veterinarian as soon as possible, ensuring that good airflow is provided, for example, make holes in a hessian bag or box or carry the animal in a cage in a well-ventilated vehicle
- dehydration—give the animal water or a weak Staminade solution or similar, then transport it to a vet for fluid therapy
- burns—these may be minor singed areas, blisters or serious open wounds. Avoid using creams or powders. Cool the burn with clean water, apply wet clean towels or sheets to the damaged area and transport to a vet.

Other consequences of bushfire are starvation and stress. Bushfire victims must be transported to a veterinarian as soon as possible after first-aid treatment. Keep the animal quiet and in the dark during transport, providing good ventilation but avoiding draughts.

Prevention Avoid using fires in bush settings, and never do so at times of high fire risk. Take note of signs indicating fire danger. Never throw burning cigarettes or matches out of car windows or along trails.

Human safety

Your first concern when contemplating the rescue of an animal must be for your own safety and the safety of other humans. In wildlife rescue situations there are a number of potential risks that need to be kept in mind and avoided:

◆ first, you could be endangering yourself when rescuing the animal
◆ second, you could be injured by the animal
◆ third, you could come in contact with a diseased animal, which potentially could transmit the disease to you.

Be aware of all three risks when rescuing and caring for wildlife. These three risk factors can largely be avoided or minimised.

When rescuing an animal from a road, for example, be sure that you don't place yourself in danger of becoming the next road victim. Do not climb trees or onto roofs to rescue an animal unless you are comfortable and capable of doing so safely.

To avoid injury from the animal, always think before you touch it. Which part of the animal is likely to be used in defence? Is it most likely to bite, kick or scratch? Immobilise the most dangerous part of the animal first; examine the handling techniques recommended in this book if you are not sure how to approach the animal. Never handle venomous snakes unless you are an expert in reptile handling.

There are some basic principles that will help to avoid or minimise the risk of disease transmission from animals to humans. Diseases that can be transmitted from animals to humans are called zoonoses or zoonotic diseases. People most at risk from infection of zoonotic diseases are those whose immune system may be compromised. This includes young children, aged people and people whose immunity is weakened through illness or medication.

Infection and disease transmission may be prevented by observing the following good handling and hygiene practices:

◆ use protective equipment, such as gloves, masks and goggles, when needed
◆ use safe handling techniques
◆ consider vaccination for tetanus if you are regularly handling wildlife (discuss this with your doctor)
◆ consider vaccination for rabies if you are regularly handling bats (discuss this with your doctor)
◆ maintain good personal hygiene. Wash your hands with an antiseptic soap before and after handling animals and inbetween handling different animals.
◆ keep high standards of hygiene in animal enclosures and disinfect regularly. Always disinfect enclosures between use by different animals
◆ clean and treat all human injuries, such as cuts and abrasions, immediately with a disinfectant such as iovone or betadine
◆ no eating, drinking or smoking in animal areas.

Note: Until more is known about the Australian bat lyssavirus, rescuers and carers should seek advice from their doctor and take adequate precautions against infection. It is also advisable to contact your doctor if you have any health concerns regarding your involvement with wildlife.

Did you know that bats see with sound?

All bats have eyes, but insectivorous bats have only very small eyes. Insectivorous bats emit ultrasonic calls. These bats then assess the position of objects by the reflection of vibrations produced by their call. They are able to navigate and locate prey without using sight. Reflection of objects is collected by large ear flaps. It is therefore said they 'see' with their ears rather than their eyes.

Catching wildlife

The catching and handling of injured wildlife should be carried out rapidly to avoid further damage or distress to the animal. Cornering the animal with the help of another person may speed up the catching process. A plan should be devised before trying to catch the animal. Decide who herds the animal and who does the actual catch. When catching animals, be quick, confident and gentle.

Many injured animals are further damaged during capture. Sometimes the animal crashes into solid objects as it tries to get away or it is hit with a capture net. Before you start catching, familiarise yourself with the correct handling technique for the species. Even if you have not handled this species before, try to be confident. Lack of confidence and hesitation often leads to injury to the handler or to the animal, or the animal may escape from the catchers.

Do not lift animals by the head or the neck; always support the weight of the animal's body. Do not hold the animal too tight as this could restrict its normal breathing. An animal that is restrained securely but gently will struggle less.

Immediately after catching, place the animal in a secure transport container, bag or cardboard box.

Transporting wildlife

Take great care when transporting injured animals. Even for a healthy wild animal this would be a stressful event. To transport wild mammals, follow these general guidelines:

- keep a constant temperature of about 25°C for adults animals and 32°C for very young animals
- no draughts, but adequate ventilation, especially in hot conditions, or use an air-conditioned vehicle
- no noise, such as shouting, laughing , a loud radio, or a dog barking
- no exhaust fumes
- one animal per bag or box (except mother and pouch young or known family group)
- avoid prolonged transport.

If animals are to travel unattended, their box should be clearly labelled: LIVE ANIMAL—KEEP AWAY FROM HEAT, COLD, RAIN OR DIRECT SUN. A name and phone number for a contact at both the dispatching and receiving ends should also be included on the label.

Note: Do not leave animals in closed vehicles.

Equipment list for animal capture
- binoculars
- nets
- gloves
- towels
- spotlight
- hessian bags
- wool sacks
- pillowslips
- cardboard boxes
- newspaper, shredded paper, straw

The stress of captivity

When rehabilitating a wild animal, a balance needs to be struck between the need to tend to the animal, the stress this may induce and the degree of tolerance to human contact that the animal should develop. Stress contributes considerably to the death rate of animals that come into captivity. The care of the animal during all stages of rehabilitation should be geared towards minimising stress.

Stress to an animal comes in many forms. Stress may be caused by inexpert or rough handling, temperature stress (over- or underheating), visual stress (seeing humans or other animals that frighten the animal), auditory stress (hearing barking dogs or other loud or strange noises), nutritional stress (the wrong food, not enough food or the wrong presentation of the right food).

Some species, such as ringtail possums or Sugar Gliders, prefer to be with others of their species and generally suffer less stress if they have company.

Did you know that when a nest falls out of a tree you can usually put it back successfully?

If the nest has completely dislodged from its original position, place the whole nest in a similar sized basket and put the basket and nest back where it was. There is a good chance that the parents will continue to care for their young.

Stress can be minimised by replicating as closely as possible the species' wild environment—the appropriate temperature, suitable company, somewhere comfortable to sleep and an enclosure that is quiet.

Rehabilitation

At all stages of rehabilitation it is important to remember the animal's final destination—back to the wild. All care of the animal should be given whilst keeping this in mind. The animal needs to stay fearful of humans if it is to survive in the wild. The housing, cleaning and feeding of the animal should therefore be done quickly, with a minimum amount of disturbance.

If an animal comes to respond to a human carer, it may approach humans and expect food when back in the wild. To avoid this, the animal in care could be familiarised only with a certain shape and colour—one that it is unlikely ever to see in the bush. For example, the carer could always wear a white lab coat when dealing with the animal. Once back in the bush, the animal is unlikely to encounter someone in a white lab coat and the sight of a human minus a white lab coat is less likely to trigger an association with food.

Release of adult wildlife

Preparation for release

Permission from the relevant State wildlife authority must be sought prior to release of the animal (contact addresses are listed in the reference section, see pages 127–8). The preparation for release of an injured or sick native animal should begin the day it comes into captivity. Wild animals should not be tamed as this will be detrimental to them when they return to the wild. A tamed wild animal behaves differently from a wild one and this often means that it is not accepted by members of its own species.

If the animal has only been in captivity for a short time—say, one or two weeks—less preparation for release will be needed, provided the animal is fit and the release site is suitable. If, however, the animal has been cared for over an extended period, a far greater amount of preparation is required to ensure a successful release.

Once the animal's health improves, it should be given more space to exercise. It is important that the animal is fit prior to release. It must be able to do whatever it normally does in the wild, such as climb, fly, swim or run.

In the weeks and days prior to release, it may also be beneficial to provide more natural foods as a complete change of diet from captive to wild may cause digestive upsets. For example, a brushtail possum that has been fed on fruit such as apple, banana and pear should be given more eucalyptus leaves, bottlebrush, wattle flowers and the like for several days at the least, prior to its release. Most books on native animals list the animals' natural food preferences.

While still in captivity, the animal should also be acclimatised to outside temperatures, particularly night temperatures. Although it is best to release wildlife as soon as possible, the adjustment to outside temperatures must be made gradually. If a possum, for example, has been living indoors for two months due to an injury, it cannot be released as soon as it is healthy but should live in an outside enclosure for at least one or two weeks.

For some social animals, such as Rainbow Lorikeets or ringtail possums, it is advantageous for them to be released in small groups. During their rehabilitation period, social animals of the same species can be kept together to provide group support, which is beneficial to them after release. For possums and gliders, it is also an advantage to provide a nest-box at the release site. Not having to compete for a place to sleep may make the difference between survival and death. Nest-boxes can be constructed as shown on page 29. Familiarise the animal with its nest-box well before its release. This may reduce the stress on the animal once it is set free.

Timing the release

The timing of release is crucial to the survival of the animal. Appropriate times for release are different for each species and some homework should be done to find out the species' seasonal behaviour.

As a general rule, the animal should not be released during the breeding season unless it has a known territory and can be returned there within one or two weeks after being taken into captivity. Ideally, the release should be timed so that it is just before or just after the breeding season. This is particularly important for territorial animals, such as magpies and kookaburras.

When releasing an animal, the time of year should also be considered. An animal that has been in captivity for an extended period should not be released in the middle of winter when the food supply is less abundant and it is more difficult for animals to gather enough food. Sometimes arrangements can be made to provide supplementary food for the released animal at the release site.

The release of migratory birds must also be timed carefully. Often a bird is only in an area during the breeding season and migrates elsewhere for winter, or vice versa. The release should be planned

---

Did you know that when a bird hits the windscreen of a car it may need your help to survive?

If the bird falls to the ground concussed, it becomes a target for predators. Stop the car, find the bird and, if only concussed, keep it in a dark and quiet place for one hour before letting it go where you found it.

---

to take place at the end of the major breeding activity, for example, one month before the birds normally migrate. The bird needs this time to build up the muscle strength required for sustained flight. The bird must also have a higher than average body weight as, during migration, its body fat reserves will be depleted.

If it is not possible to release the bird before migration, it should be kept in captivity until its species returns in the next season. The bird should then be released just after the return of the birds to the area. In the general confusion of many birds arriving at the same time, its chances of establishing itself are better.

The time of day is also important to consider when planning the release. Nocturnal animals should be released just after dark. For animals active in the day, early morning would be the most suitable time to release them. This gives the animal the maximum number of waking hours to settle in and find somewhere safe to sleep.

Animals should be released only in the area close to where they were found.

Genetic variation exists between different populations of animals of the same species and releasing the animal close to where it came from reduces the risk of interfering with the genetics of a population. If the animal was found on a major road, study a map of the area to locate a park or urban bushland area nearby that is suitable.

If the release site is a national park or the responsibility of another land management organisation, the local authorities should be asked for permission to release the animal. During transport to the release site it is preferable not to travel during the heat of the day. The animal should be kept warm, dark and quiet in a cardboard box, hessian sack or calico bag during transport.

Euthanasia

When an animal is suffering or has no chance of surviving its release back into the wild due to the injuries it has received, euthanasia—putting the animal down humanely—may be the kindest thing for it. The most appropriate form of euthanasia—the method that causes least distress to the animal—is by injection of a barbiturate overdose. Only qualified people are allowed to administer this solution under the authority of a veterinarian.

No other form of euthanasia is recommended for wildlife. For example, exhaust fumes may burn the animal severely before killing it. Driving over an animal can break its bones without actually killing it. Nor is freezing of a reptile or frog an acceptable form of euthanasia. The formation of ice crystals on the skin and in the tissues is likely to cause significant pain while the animal is still conscious. Decapitation of reptiles is also not recommended as unconsciousness in the severed head is not immediate.

Handling
AND EMERGENCY CARE FOR
COMMON MAMMAL GROUPS

General points

The following information on housing and diet is appropriate for maintaining animals for one to three days. Diets would need to be changed for longer periods in captivity, for example, minerals and vitamins may need to be added and a more varied diet may be required. When the rescuer is caring for the animal over an extended period, it is recommended that information on more precise dietary and housing requirements be sought. For more detailed specifications on the longer-term care of native wildlife, consult your State wildlife authority (these are listed in the reference section on pages 127–8). State wildlife authorities will be able to refer you to organisations that are familiar with wildlife care.

In most States you will need a licence from the State wildlife authority to care for a native animal (bird, mammal or reptile). In most cases, you are also obliged to return the animal to the wild once it can fend for itself.

Housing sick animals

Critically ill animals require intensive-care housing. These animals need to be kept in accommodation that allows them to stretch out comfortably but restricts their movement. The housing should also be small to avoid the need to chase and catch the animal for every treatment or check-up. A small enclosure at this stage will also prevent the animal from wasting its energy searching for food or water or marking its scent.

During intensive care, the animal should be kept in dark and quiet surroundings at a constant temperature suitable to the species and age of the animal. Once the animal's condition is stable, it can be moved to some slightly larger accommodation.

Some guidelines for larger temporary accommodation are given below for each animal group. Artificial heating can be reduced once the animal's health stabilises. An adult animal in a stable condition should be able to maintain its body temperature.

The animal should be given clean, dry

bedding material daily and clean fresh water should be available at all times. Most animals will need privacy to feel secure. This can be achieved by including a nest-box or a screen, such as a towel draped over the cage or a pile of leaves inside the cage under which the animal can hide.

Temperature

Temperature requirements vary between species and within species depending on the age and health status of the animal. The best way to know you are providing the correct temperature for an individual is by observing it. A shivering animal is too cold, a panting animal is too hot. The animal should feel comfortably warm to touch.

Animals of some species, such as insectivorous bats and pygmy possums, go into a state of torpor and should be given access to temperatures low enough to allow for this once they are healthy. Torpor should be avoided in sick animals, as this slows down the metabolic rate, suppresses the immune system and may increase bacterial growth. The following ambient temperatures may be used as a general guide:

- healthy adults, 25°C (or ambient temperatures)
- sick/injured adult, 28°C
- furless young, 35°C
- furred young, 32°C
- weaned young, 28°C

Whenever the condition of the animal allows, the heat source should provide a temperature gradient. The animal can then find its own preferred temperature within the enclosure by moving closer or further away from the heat source. Heat can be provided by wrapped hotwater bottles, heat lamps, heaters (no exposed flames) and heating pads.

Care for specific mammals

Platypuses

Handling Platypuses that require care are often 'dispersing young', that is, they have recently left the mother. They might be found either in water or on dry land. They can be lifted by the tail but care should be taken as the males have a poisonous spur on their hind legs. The animal can be transported in a box filled with straw or leaf litter. Temperatures above

Exceptions to the temperature guidelines given above include the following:		
Species	Healthy	Sick or injured
Platypus	maximum 25°C	maximum 25°C
Echidna	maximum 25°C	maximum 25°C
Insectivorous bat	ambient temperature	25°C
Mountain Pygmy-Possum	10°–22°C	maximum 22°C

25°C must be avoided as a Platypus cannot regulate its own temperature above this and may die of heat stress.

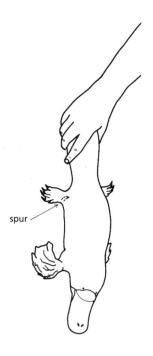

spur

Platypuses can be lifted by the tail but care should be taken as the males have a poisonous spur on the hind legs.

Temporary accommodation and feeding requirements For Platypuses, these are very specialised. They need a large waterbody for feeding, a tunnel system and nest boxes. They also need to be fed a variety of live foods, such as yabbies and worms, which are difficult to obtain. This species is best transported to an institution, such as a large zoo, that is equipped and trained in its care and has

specialised Platypus holding facilities. The Platypus' chances of survival may be significantly compromised unless it is given specialised care.

Echidnas

Handling Grasp the animal's back legs with gloved hands or gently lift it with a blunt-ended stick placed under the body. Alternatively, cover the animal with a very thick towel or blanket and lift it carefully into a transport container.

An echidna can be handled by gently holding the animal's back legs. Alternatively it can be lifted with one hand under its belly which has no spines.

If the animal has wedged itself into a tight spot or dug itself into the ground, allow it to come out of its own accord. Echidnas use this technique as a defence mechanism and forcing the animal out could injure it. A sturdy wooden box or garbage bin can be used to transport echidnas. Echidnas are excellent escapists and good climbers.

Accommodation   Echidnas can be housed in a dig-proof enclosure with straw or leaf litter on the floor. Avoid wire enclosures unless the bottom 30 cm is covered with plastic or perspex to prevent injuries to the snout of the animal. Ensure that the animal can avoid high temperatures by providing shaded areas.

Feeding   The echidna can be fed high-protein gruel made from the following ingredients and mixed well:
400g finely minced meat (beef)
50g wheat bran
150g Glucodin
2 raw eggs
30mL olive oil
5g Caco 3 (calcium carbonate)
5mL Equine E (vitamin E)
600mL water
Some logs with termites in them can also be placed in the enclosure.

Carnivorous marsupials (dasyurids)

Handling   Large native cats (quolls) and Tasmanian Devils have very powerful jaws and are capable of inflicting a significant injury. They can be handled

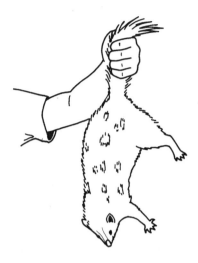

Large carnivorous marsupials can be handled by the tail and transferred to a hessian sack for transport.

by the tail (close to where the tail meets the body) and the back legs lifted off the ground. If the animal is kept in gentle motion it will spread its legs and remain relatively calm. At this stage the animal can be 'swung', gently but quickly, into a hessian or cloth bag. Tasmanian Devils will need a hessian bag. Care should be taken that the animal does not bite the handler through the bag.

For capturing the smaller species insert your hand into a calico bag and grasp the animal through the bag, then turn the bag inside out, leaving the animal in the bag.

Temporary accommodation   The larger species of dasyurid can be kept in aviaries but bird-wire netting may not strong enough to restrain Tasmanian Devils as they will chew their way out of most enclosures. They will need a chain-linked or weld-mesh enclosure. Wooden doors or frames will be chewed so it is best to use an enclosure with a steel pipe frame.

A large aquarium with sand or leaf litter over the bottom and a lid or cover made from flywire in a solid frame is suitable for the smaller species. Many small dasyurids use sand for bathing. Fine sand of good quality is used for this purpose and may need to be collected from a semi-arid area as it is not always available for sale.

Concrete or other abrasive surfaces should be avoided for all dasyurids as they may cause sore feet. Fine sand or leaf litter make suitable surfaces.

These animals like sun-basking, so access to an open area should preferably be given. Nest-boxes, hollow logs or a drainage pipe of an appropriate size should be provided for privacy. The climbing species of dasyurids, such as the Spotted-tailed Quoll, need climbing structures such as branches.

Feeding A good quality commercial cat food can be combined with whole small animals, such as rats, mice and chicken with bones or skin, to provide roughage. The small species, such as Kowari, dunnarts and planigales, like to eat mealworms, earthworms, grubs and insects. Avoid feeding them raw meat because of the risk of infection. This is especially important with mutton, which has been linked with a disorder fatal to dasyurids.

Do you know the specific names for the 'babies' of some species?

Young bird	chick
Unfledged bird, (usually a pigeon)	squab
Young dog	pup
Young eagle	eaglet
Newborn eel	elver
Young goose	gosling
Young hawk or hen	chicken
Young kangaroo	joey
Young rodent	pup
Newborn shark or young seal	pup
Young whale, cow or camel	calf
Young swan	cygnet
Small fish	fry
Immature hen	pullet
Immature rooster	cockerel
Young owl	owlet
Salmon offspring	smolt
Young hare	leveret
Young cat or rabbit	kitten
Young fox	cub
Young deer	fawn
Young horse	foal
Young pig	piglet

Bandicoots

Handling Bandicoots should not be handled by the tail. They can be grasped around the neck and shoulders while simultaneously restraining the back legs, taking care not to restrict breathing. Alternatively, a towel or cloth can be thrown over the animal prior to handling it. They will shed fur in a defence gesture.

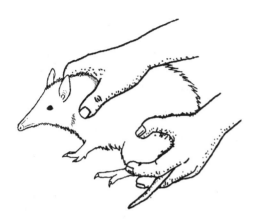

Bandicoots can be grasped firmly around the neck and shoulders, taking care not to restrict breathing while simultaneously restraining the back legs.

The animal should be transferred to a sack or straw-filled box for transport as soon as possible.

Temporary accommodation Bandicoots are solitary and nocturnal. Enclosures must be dog-proof and measures should be taken to prevent the animal from burrowing out at the edges. Some dense cover at ground level is essential for security—the animal will panic if such cover is not available. Provide grass tussocks if possible. Alternatively, branches can be tied together in bunches and several bunches can be leaned against each other to make good shelter. Some bandicoots will burrow into a deep straw layer.

A soil floor is good for these animals as they will dig for insects. They should not be kept on wire or concrete as this will damage their feet. A concrete yard can be used provided it is covered with a thick layer of straw or similar material.

Feeding Most bandicoots are omnivorous, eating both meat and plant material, but they have a preference for a carnivorous diet. Dog kibble can be given but it may need to be soaked first. Try small amounts of cooked meat and various fruits to encourage feeding. Insects, snails, grubs, mealworms, grasshoppers or fly pupae can also be offered, as well as a few scoops of fresh soil daily.

Koalas

Handling Wild Koalas might be cute but are certainly not cuddly—they intensely resent handling and may bite and scratch. Koalas in need of care can be caught from trees using the following technique. At least two people are needed. One person holds a bag. One person uses a long-handled fishing rod or extension pole with a rag attached to it. The pole is used to touch the Koala on the head to encourage it to come down the tree. It is important to keep it moving. When it reaches the level of the second person's shoulder height, a bag is quickly wrapped around the animal, almost 'walking' the animal backwards into the bag. Then the animal's front legs are secured and the head is pushed into the bag.

Koalas can be handled from behind by the upper arms and temporarily transported in hessian sacks. Alternatively, an inexperienced handler may find it safer to throw a blanket over the animal prior to handling. Over longer distances,

A sturdy forked tree makes a good Koala perch.

as several thick, upright, forked tree-trunks of different sizes. Minimal human interference is important as wild Koalas become stressed very easily with human attention and handling.

Feeding   Considerable expertise in eucalypt identification is necessary, so the animal is best transferred to an organisation that is familiar with the care of Koalas. Koalas only eat *Eucalyptus* leaves. These must be offered to the animal when fresh and with plenty of new shoots. At least two of the following staple species of eucalypt should be offered fresh daily for feeding: *Eucalyptus nicholii*, narrow-leaved black peppermint; *E. viminalis*, manna gum; *E. scoparia*,

transport the Koala in a large, darkened box with a stout branch on which it can perch. During short journeys (less than two hours), the Koala could be transported in a hessian bag provided it is in an air-conditioned vehicle.

Temporary accommodation   Very sick Koalas are kept indoors in a room with stout perches or, if they are unable to climb, they can be kept in a plastic washing basket lined with padded material. A thick towel or similar material can be rolled up and placed at one end of the basket as a 'pretend' limb that the animal may wish to hold onto.

For animals that can maintain their body temperature and can climb, aviary-style accommodation is suitable in the short term. Provide good perches, such

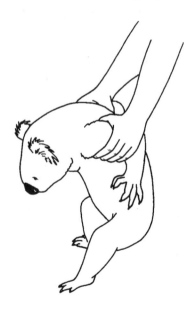

Koalas can be picked up by the upper arms from behind. An inexperienced handler may be safer throwing a blanket over the animal prior to handling.

Wallangarra white gum; *E. o ata*, swamp gum; *E. goniocalyx*, long-leaved box gum; *E. tereticornis*, forest red gum; *E. camaldulensis*, river red gum; *E. robusta*, swamp mahogany; *E. grandis*, flooded gum; *E. punctata*, grey gum; *E. maculata*, spotted gum.

Several of any of the following can also be offered: *E. camphora*, mountain swamp gum; *E. cypellocarpa*, mountain grey gum; *E. radiata*, narrow-leaved peppermint gum; *E. obliqua*, messmate stringybark; *E. botryoides*, southern mahogany; *E. saligna*, Sydney blue gum; *E. microcorys*, tallowwood; *E. haemastoma*, scribbly gum; *E sideroxylon*, red ironbark; *E. pilularis*, coastal blackbutt.

Leaves should be collected from an area where they have not been contaminated with exhaust fumes or sprayed with chemicals. The leaves must be kept in water at all times and discarded once they dry out. Koalas will rather starve than eat anything less than fresh excellent-quality leaves from species that they like to eat. In addition to checking the leaves for signs of the Koala feeding, the faecal output can be monitored. A Koala that is eating sufficiently is expected to produce between 100 and 150 faecal pellets per day.

Wombats

Handling Wombats can be difficult to handle as they can be aggressive and are sometimes extremely heavy. First, try encouraging them to run into a large sack or stout box. Alternatively, they can be grasped from behind around the

Wombats can be grasped around the shoulders from behind, but care must be taken as they can bite savagely.

shoulders, but they can bite savagely and extreme care must be taken that the animal's teeth face away from the handler. The animal can also scratch with its powerful claws and these claws must also face away from the handler.

Temporary accommodation An enclosed, paved courtyard is suitable in the short term. Wombats should not be kept for more than a few days without being able to burrow unless they are very ill. A yard with a natural dirt floor is preferable but the fence line must be burrow-proof. Fences should be set in the ground at least 30 cm and be at least 1.5 m high, or higher if chain-link fence is used.

Some form of security burrow should be provided, such as a stout box or a length of cement pipe. The animal also needs shade to avoid high temperatures.

Feeding Good quality hay, vegetables and a concentrate such as horse-pellets are suitable.

Possums and gliders

Handling Possums and gliders are readily handled by the tail, while the neck and shoulder region is grasped simultaneously. Hessian sacks or straw-filled boxes are adequate for transport.

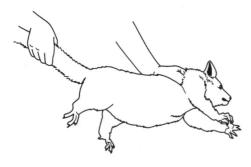

Possums and gliders can be handled by the tail while the neck and shoulder region is grasped simultaneously.

Temporary accommodation An aviary with nesting areas and climbing structures can be used. Nest-boxes or hollow logs, blocked at one end and placed above the ground, can be used for nesting. Ringtail possums in the wild make a nest, called a drey, from branches and twigs. They can be given a 'pretend' drey made from two wire hanging-plant baskets and fibre liners to form a sphere. The two baskets can be joined with

wire ties. Branches and ropes can be used for climbing.

Feeding A wide variety of fruits and vegetables should be offered. Native fruits and flowers, for example, grevillea, melaleuca (tea-tree) and callistemon (bottlebrush), are appreciated. Ringtail possums normally eat large quantities of leaves so gum leaves and tips and other native vegetation should be provided. Greater Gliders are almost exclusively leaf eaters so the feeding practices outlined for Koalas (pages 68–9) should be followed. Smaller Sugar Gliders, pygmy possums, Feathertail Gliders and Leadbeater's Possums have a higher protein diet that is provided by insects and pollen in the wild.

A high-protein, high-energy gruel should be provided in small quantities as a supplement. For example, mix the following ingredients in a blender for two minutes to make a palatable and balanced feed. This mix can be stored in the refrigerator.

25g Heinz high-protein baby cereal
1 hard-boiled egg
1 teaspoon Sustagen
150mL honey
150mL warm water

Large kangaroos and wallabies

Handling Kangaroos are highly strung, panic easily and may sustain further injury if handled incorrectly. Large kangaroos can be particularly dangerous during catching and handling. Capture must be as quick as possible to avoid the

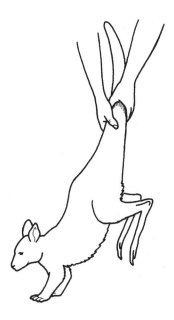

Small wallabies and rat kangaroos can be quickly picked up by the base of the tail and then transferred to a hessian bag.

animal suffering from heat exhaustion, running into fences or otherwise harming itself.

The capture techniques below assume the animal is injured and can therefore be approached. For more mobile animals, large capture nets or other techniques may be needed. A large blanket or wool sack is a useful tool of restraint. This can be thrown over the animal and gently pulled around it, allowing the animal to be moved safely to a car for transport. Alternatively, the animal can be caught and restrained by the tail before being transferred to a hessian sack.

Most kangaroos and wallabies will relax once left undisturbed and suspended in a darkened sack. Large kangaroos must

be placed in such a way that they don't injure themselves when kicking out during transport. A wool sack can be used for the larger species and a hessian bag or straw-filled box for small species.

If kangaroos are to be transported over a long distance, a box is an appropriate container. The transport box should be well ventilated and allow the animal to stand on all fours and turn around. As the animal may jump, to avoid damage to the head and neck the box should have a flexible mesh ceiling, which can be padded on the inside.

Most kangaroos and wallabies fare better during transport after the administration of a tranquilliser, prescribed by a veterinarian.

Temporary accommodation   Kangaroos and wallabies must be housed in enclosures with two-metre-high fences. These enclosures should have no internal sharp projections or corners and no loose wires; they should be dog-proof and lined with opaque material, such as hessian. Provide some shelter from extreme weather conditions. Avoid concrete as this may cause abrasion on the feet. Enclosures with natural soil or grass floors are preferable.

Feeding   The animal should be fed under cover and the area should be kept scrupulously clean. A good quality hay or lucerne chaff and small amounts of concentrated stock feed (kangaroo or dairy cubes) are adequate. Carrots can also be offered. Many kangaroo species like to eat some tree bark, particularly stringybarks. Provide some logs in the enclosure that still has the bark on the trunk. These are good for the maintenance of teeth and gums.

Small wallabies and rat kangaroos

Handling These animals can be picked up quickly and firmly at the base of the tail and transferred to a hessian bag or a deep box filled with straw or hay. Avoid holding these animals by the tail for any length of time. Thrashing about by the animal may result in spinal damage. If a bag is used to contain the animal, it should be suspended during transport since the animal will try to jump about if placed on a solid surface. Attempts to restrain the animal by holding the body must be avoided as this may lead to loss of large amounts of fur. Shedding of fur is a normal protective escape mechanism for these animals.

Temporary accommodation Enclosures must be fully fenced and dog-proof. The fence should be approximately two metres high, and care should be taken that the animal cannot burrow out at the edges. Most of these species rely on vegetative cover for safety. Some dense cover at ground level is essential for security and the animal will panic if such cover is not available. These animals will appreciate hollow logs or nest-boxes for privacy. Another good shelter can be made from bunches of branches tied up and leaning together. Some

rat-kangaroo species will burrow into a deep straw layer. The animals will also use straw as a nesting material.

Feeding Food can be similar to that given to larger wallabies and kangaroos but with higher protein, such as a very small amount of dog kibble added, and greater variety, such as assorted chopped vegetables.

Flying foxes

Handling Current health information concerning lyssavirus indicates that people could be at risk from infection if bitten or scratched by an infected bat. Saliva and blood from an infected bat can also infect humans if this material contacts broken skin. Contact your doctor for further information.

Leather gloves are recommended to prevent bites or scratches. As flying

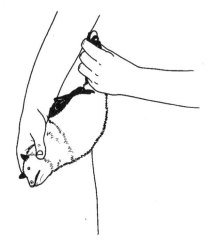

Flying foxes can bite severely. They should be grasped behind the head while the claws are gently removed from whatever they are holding.

foxes can bite severely, these are best grasped behind the head. Gently remove the claws from whatever they are holding. Then wrap the animal loosely in a cloth leaving the head protruding and allowing the hind feet to grip onto something. Flying foxes can be transported in a cage or box with a widely spaced wire-mesh top so that the animal can hang comfortably. Alternatively, strong sticks can be secured across the top of a box to enable the animal to hang.

Temporary accommodation An aviary, with several high perches and shelter from the weather, is suitable. Enclosures for flying foxes must have both full sun and full shade available.

Feeding In the short term, a wide variety of soft fruits cut into small pieces can be offered. This should be supplemented with Wombaroo sprinkled on the fruit. Alternatively, a high-protein and calcium mix such as Complan may be used. The food container should be hung from the walls or roof of the aviary in such a way that the animal can hang comfortably while feeding.

Small insectivorous bats (microchiropterans)

These animals are often mistaken for baby fruit bats. They can usually be distinguished by the finer fur, small eyes, more complex facial features, such as skin flaps around the nose, and by the presence of a tail. (See page 108 for the distinction between fruit bats and insectivorous bats.)

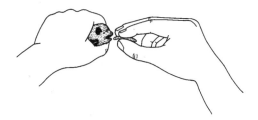

While hand-feeding an insectivorous bat, envelop the animal in the hand allowing only its head to protrude.

Handling Note the earlier warning regarding lyssavirus. Insectivorous bats are best handled with gloves. Handle them gently in a cupped hand and transport them in calico bags. They should be kept insulated from extremes of temperature and kept quiet. Transport them in an esky with either a wrapped hotwater bottle or an ice brick depending on the ambient temperature. Healthier bats can be kept in ambient temperatures but a sick or injured bat should be transported at approximately 25°C.

Temporary accommodation A small enclosure, such as a cardboard box with towelling or some other material pinned on the inner 'wall', is suitable for holding these animals during convalescence. Alternatively, a wire frame measuring 30cm by 30cm covered with fine netting is suitable in the short term. Pin some folds of material to the inside wall in which the animal can roost. Cover the netted enclosure with a towel or cloth. For longer-term care, a well-sealed shade house with a bat roost should be provided.

Feeding   Most insectivorous bats take insects on the wing and must therefore learn to recognise food in dishes. Generally, hand feeding is necessary for the first few days in captivity. A high protein, high energy paste made from equal parts of high protein baby cereal, Digestelac, honey and water can be offered on the end of a small brush. Insects such as mealworms, fly pupae or moths may be eaten when offered with a pair of forceps. The animals should be warmed in the hand before feeding and then kept warm for about two hours after feeding to facilitate digestion. Leave a small dish containing mealworms in the enclosure to encourage the bats to feed themselves.

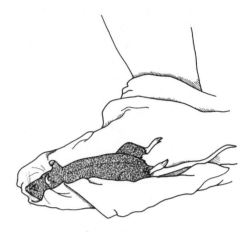

Handling rodents: a hand is inserted into a calico bag, the animal is grasped through the bag and the bag is then turned inside out, leaving the animal inside.

Native rats and mice (rodents)

Handling   These animals are best handled by the 'calico bag' technique as outlined for the carnivorous marsupials (page 65).

Temporary accommodation   Aquaria make good enclosures for the smaller rodent species. A well-fitting lid that allows for adequate ventilation is suitable. A metal-framed lid covered in metal flywire can be used. Wood will be chewed by these species. Provide clean sand or leaf litter in the aquarium into which they can burrow. Avoid coarse sand as this could damage the animal's feet. Water-rats can be housed in aviary-style accommodation provided it is burrow-proof. Water-rats will need a nest-box and a small body of water, such as a wading pool, with easy exit and entry ramps.

Feeding   Rat and mouse cubes, available from pet shops, are appropriate foods for most native rats and mice. These should be supplemented with a variety of seeds (canary), grasses, fruits and vegetables.

The large water-rat is carnivorous and should be offered fish. Canned dog or cat food can be used for a few days if no fresh fish is available.

Handling
AND EMERGENCY CARE FOR COMMON BIRD GROUPS

The information in this chapter applies to cases of emergency care only. The housing and dietary guidelines outlined are adequate to maintain birds for a period of one or two days. Diets would need to be changed for longer periods in captivity; minerals and vitamins may need to be added and a more varied diet introduced. When the rescuer must care for the bird over an extended period, it is recommended that more information is obtained on precise dietary and housing requirements. The reference section (pages 127–8) lists contact numbers where such information can be obtained from wildlife authorities in each State.

A basic but very important rule to remember is never to hold birds tightly around the chest. Birds cannot breathe unless they can expand their chest. Restraint must be firm but never squeeze a bird as it will only struggle more when it is being suffocated.

Capturing an injured wild bird should be done rapidly as prolonged pursuits will cause damage and distress. A fishing net for large birds or a butterfly net for smaller species is useful, and a cloth or towel that can be thrown over the bird. When catching a wild bird, evaluate the situation and consider herding it to a place where it might be more easily caught, such as a corner of a fenced yard or a garage. Work in a catching team of two or more people if possible, as an animal can then be driven into an area where it can be caught. While collecting birds from the shoreline, place yourself between the water's edge and the bird to avoid the animal returning to the water.

The equipment for catching birds includes:

- long-handled fishing nets and butter-fly nets
- pillowslips and cloth bags
- gloves and goggles
- towels and blankets
- torch.

The following is a summary of 'dos and don'ts' when handling birds:

- do wear protective gear such as gloves and goggles

- do take special care with birds such as herons and egrets as they may cause damage to a handler's eyes
- do hold birds at waist level to avoid injury to face or eyes
- don't lift birds by the head or neck—always support the weight of the animal's body
- don't hold birds too tightly as you may restrict normal breathing
- don't ever approach with your face and eyes too close to a box or bag with a bird in it as some birds will stab.

If an adult wild bird allows itself to be caught easily it is usually quite ill. It is best to observe an uninjured but apparently helpless young bird for at least half an hour before picking it up. Young birds that have just left the nest often look rather helpless and abandoned. Just like humans do not learn to walk and run in a day, so young birds go through an 'awkward' stage.

Young birds that appear abandoned are frequently picked up by people unnecessarily. The parents are often not

Young birds that have fallen from the nest can be placed back into an artificial nest in the same tree or bush. The parents are quite likely to find the youngster and continue to care for it.

far away and may return to care for their offspring shortly. Far too many young birds are 'rescued' unnecessarily only to die later as a result of inadequate care. If, after examination, the young bird is found to be uninjured, it should be returned to the spot where it was found or placed in the bushes near the nest if this can be located. If the bird is in danger of cat or dog attack, it may be placed in a container or box (not too deep otherwise the bird can't get out when its parents return) and hung in a tree or bush. The container should be sheltered from direct sunlight and heavy rain. The parents are quite likely to find the bird and will almost certainly continue to feed it. Stay around to ensure that predators are kept away and the parents do return. If they don't, the bird will need to be taken into care.

During transport the bird must be kept warm, quiet, dark and protected from draught. Do not transport animals in the boot of a car as carbon monoxide poisoning or suffocation may occur.

Transport

Transportation is a stressful event for a wild, injured bird (the strange environment, noise, motion, and so on). Many animals die during transportation due to stress or further injuries sustained during the journey. The main causes of mortality during transport are stress, temperature extremes and injuries. Wild animals should be transported quickly and with a minimum of stress.

The transport container should house the animal in reasonable comfort for the entire journey and should:

- be escape-proof
- be weather and leak-proof
- allow adequate ventilation
- have no sharp edges or protrusions
- have a perch or bedding.

The box should be fitted with a perch for perching birds or lined with a towel or similar for gripping. The box should be large enough for the animal to stand upright, but not too large as the animal may be thrown around and become injured. A bag of natural material, such as cotton, can be used for nearly all birds. Birds will settle well during transport if suspended in a bag in the vehicle. This way it is unlikely that the bird will injure itself by thrashing or flapping. (Transport in bags should only be used for short journeys during cool conditions.) Pillowslips or similar soft bags can be used.

Rehabilitation

The bird should be provided with clean, dry bedding daily and clean, fresh water should be available at all times (straw or hay should not be used with birds as it may predispose respiratory illness). Most birds require privacy to feel secure. This can be provided by a screen such as a towel draped over the cage, or leaves behind which the bird can hide.

Birds whose temperature is below the normal range of 39°–41°C should be kept indoors at an ambient temperature of about 25°C. Indoor pens can be constructed of cloth- or hessian-covered wire, plywood, fibreglass or other materials. Netting or shade cloth can be used to cover the top of the pen. Pens can be made of a variety of materials, and in many shapes and sizes, but they all must:

* be large enough to allow the bird to stand up and stretch its wings and neck freely
* have no sharp protrusions internally or externally
* offer protection from draughts and predators
* allow adequate ventilation and light.

Some social species, such as ducks, gulls and terns, can be housed together if they are alert and their condition is stable. Weak and debilitated birds should be housed on their own to avoid stress caused by aggressive behaviour of others, and to avoid the transmission of pathogens between sick and well birds. Birds of solitary species should also be housed individually. Egrets, herons and other similar birds must have suitably sized perches in their pen. Birds with very limited mobility on land, such as grebes, must be provided with a clean rubber foam floor covering to prevent bruising and damage to the sternum.

Temperature

Normal body temperature for birds is 39°–41°C. Temperature requirements vary between species and within species, depending on age and status of the individual. The best way to judge the correct temperature for an individual is by observing it. A fluffed-up bird is too cold; a panting bird holding its wings out is too hot. The following temperatures may be used as a general guide:

* healthy adults, ambient temperature
* sick/injured adults, 25°C
* naked young (featherless), 36°C
* feathered young (downy), 27°C
* fledglings, 25°C.

When the animal's condition allows, the heat sources should provide a temperature gradient, allowing the animal to find its preferred temperature range by moving closer to or away from the heat source. Heat can be provided by hot-water bottles, heat lamps, heaters (no exposed flames or blower-type heaters) or heating pads. A shallow dish of water in the enclosure will assist in maintaining the correct humidity levels.

Common preventable diseases

The stress of captivity may predispose birds to disease. Many diseases can be prevented by good husbandry and hygiene. The following diseases are some common examples:

Aspergillosis This is a fungal disease, principally of the respiratory system. Diagnosis is very difficult as the signs vary from just 'looking fluffed' to severe

Did you know that the Peregrine Falcon is the fastest bird on Earth?

It can reach speeds of more than 300km per hour as it swoops on its prey. Peregrine Falcons attack and kill small- to medium-sized birds that fly out in the open. Many other bird species panic when they see a Peregrine Falcon, either seeking shelter or uttering cries to alarm others in the flock.

respiratory distress and death. This disease is frequently seen in seabirds that have recently come into captivity and/or are under stress. Treatment is rarely successful, therefore prevention is important. Strict hygiene, clean, dry enclosures, minimal stress and suitable husbandry techniques are important preventative measures. Hay and straw support the growth of this fungus and should not be used in enclosures.

Bacterial infections   Poor hygiene can predispose animals to bacterial infections, such as salmonellosis or pasteurellosis. Healthy wild birds carry bacteria which, under the stresses of captivity, can cause disease. Strict hygiene for food and enclosures and the isolation of sick birds may help prevent outbreaks of infections. Diagnosis and treatment require the services of an experienced veterinarian. Note that bacterial infections such as salmonellosis can be transmitted to humans—hands should be washed thoroughly after handling all birds.

Bumblefoot   This is often seen in waterbirds and raptors that are kept on inappropriate floor coverings or perches. In the wild, waterbirds do not spend much time standing, but they often do in captivity. They develop lesions on their feet that can become very large, fleshy growths infected with bacteria. The condition can be prevented by keeping birds on clean rubber matting. Bumblefoot can also be caused by unsuitable perches, such as metal rods or very smooth wood. Perches should be of varying thicknesses and made from natural branches.

Parasites   Many wild birds carry low levels of intestinal parasites. Stress can compromise the birds' immune systems, allowing previously benign burdens to cause disease. The parasites include many helminths and protozoa, which can be detected by the microscopic examination of faeces. This should be carried out routinely on all birds being rehabilitated. Parasitic outbreaks are prevented by strict hygiene for food and enclosures and the isolation and treatment of affected birds.

Specific problems

Broken limbs

First aid   Birds often sustain broken limbs by crashing into objects or from attacks by predators. If you suspect a wing or leg is broken or especially if you can see bone sticking out of the skin, the animal should be taken to a veterinarian without delay. Broken limbs must be set in place correctly by a veterinarian. Incorrect splinting of a broken wing would mean that the bird would be unlikely to fly again. Fractures that are treated immediately will have a greater chance of healing well. The bird should be handled as little as possible but the limb should be immobilised to avoid further injury. As the bird flaps about with a broken wing, it may cause more damage to blood vessels, muscle and nerves around the fracture site. Avoid using anything to immobilise the limb that will be difficult to remove. The vet will need to remove the splint for assessment of the injury, such as the taking of X-rays. Self-adhering bandage such as Vet-wrap, available from veterinarians, is ideal as it sticks to itself and not to feathers. Masking tape can be used but may cause damage to the feathers.

For leg fractures, a splint can be made from a paddlepop stick, match, or any suitably sized smooth stick. Put some padding between the splint and the leg and tape the splint to the leg. Wings can be strapped by carefully wrapping a figure-of-eight bandage around the bird. The wings should be strapped in their naturally folded position against the bird's body. The figure-of-eight bandage goes right around the body, crossing over both on the bird's chest and back. Make sure that the bird can still breathe freely. Alternatively, to prevent further damage to the injured limb, the whole bird, excluding its head, can be loosely wrapped in a towel or cloth during transport.

Further basic first-aid procedures should be followed and the bird placed in a box for transport to a veterinarian.

Prevention Refer to the information in the section on predators (page 82) and flying into windows (opposite).

Feather damage

First aid Feather damage can be caused by predators—the bird got away but the feathers didn't—or by the bird crashing into objects such as windows or cars. This is common in wild bird casualties and may significantly influence whether or not the bird can be released. Severely damaged feathers may need to be removed by a vet so that growth of new feathers is stimulated. Only a few feathers should be removed at a time. If no new growth is evident after a few weeks, no more feathers should be removed. For some species of raptor (birds of prey), such as the peregrine falcon, the removal of feathers is not recommended as new feathers may not develop to the quality needed for hunting. In such cases, it is possible to glue new feathers into the shaft of the old feather prior to release. This is called 'feather imping' and is a specialist job, best carried out by an experienced raptor rehabilitator.

In emergency situations, the broken feather quills of a growing feather, which may bleed profusely, can be removed by pulling them out in the direction of the growth. The feather should be removed by grasping it close to the skin and pulling firmly on the shaft of the feather. The bleeding will stop shortly afterwards.

Feathers that are completely removed from the feather follicle will regrow immediately. If the feather was not completely removed from the follicle it will not regrow until the bird's next moult.

Prevention Refer to the information in the section on predators (page 82) and the next section on flying into windows and objects.

Flying into windows

First aid Often the bird is only stunned and may recover quickly to be released within the hour. If the bird shows an unusual bulge somewhere on the body that is soft and filled with air, this could mean that there is some damage to an air sac. This needs to be treated by a veterinarian. In the meantime, the bird should be prevented from flapping as this will pump more air into the site. Wrap it loosely in cloth and leave the head protruding.

If internal injury or damage to the nervous system is suspected, the bird will need to be taken to a veterinary surgeon immediately.

Prevention Make windows more obvious to birds by placing stickers and pictures on them. Closed curtains or blinds will also prevent birds from crashing into the glass. If a bird is seen attacking a window repeatedly, shade should be provided over the outside of the window to stop reflections. It is thought that the bird mistakes its own reflection for an intruder in its territory. The shade should be left in place

throughout the breeding season, which might be only a few weeks or months.

Oil pollution

First aid Oil immediately destroys the waterproofing of birds' feathers. This is followed by internal problems as birds ingest the oil while attempting to preen the substance off their feathers. When a bird is caught, it should be prevented from ingesting further oil. This may be done by wiping the bill clean and loosely wrapping the bird in cloth, leaving only the head exposed. If the bird is to be transported to another site for cleaning, allow adequate ventilation as fumes from the oil may cause further illness. Birds suffering from oil pollution are often severely dehydrated and may have an abnormal body temperature.

Cleaning should not commence until the condition of the bird is satisfactory. That means that the bird's body temperature should be approximately 39°C–41°C and the bird should look bright and alert without any signs of dehydration or toxicity. Signs of toxicity include holding the head at a strange angle or unsteadiness.

Cleaning oiled birds is a specialist job and should only be undertaken if no expert help is available. Contact your local wildlife authority for advice. If no expert assistance can be found, oiled birds can be bathed in a solution of dishwashing liquid (one per cent detergent to 99 per cent warm water) at a maximum temperature of 40°C. One person is needed to hold the bird while another agitates the plumage in the solution. The bird must then be rinsed thoroughly in warm water using a shower nozzle. This process will need to be repeated several times until no oil or detergent is left in the bird's feathers. Throughout the cleaning process, utmost care must be taken not to damage the delicate structure of the feathers. Do not rub the feathers together but gently agitate them in the water.

After rinsing, excess water should be removed with a clean cloth and the bird dried near a heat source, taking care not to overheat the bird. Where possible, provide the heat source in such a way that the bird can move closer to or further away from the heat at will. Drying outside in the sun is acceptable so long as the bird is protected from predators and some shade is provided over one corner of the cage or box.

Treatment for the possible internal effects of oil pollution should only be undertaken after consultation with a veterinarian.

Prevention Increased safety measures should be imposed during transportation of large quantities of pollutant oils. Citizens can express their concern over this issue to the appropriate authorities. Boat owners and boat operators should never discharge oil in waterways. Householders should never pour oil down a sink or drain but discard these substances in sealed containers at waste collection centres.

Predation

First aid Birds are commonly the victims of attack by cats and dogs. Wounds must be treated if they are to heal well. Bathe the wound with a warm iodine solution or with warm salt water. Approximately half a teaspoon of salt in a cup of water can be used. Warm water can help the bird to avoid chilling. Clean dirt and feathers away from the wound. Pluck damaged feathers away from the wound in the direction of the feather growth, taking care not to make the bleeding worse. Deep-penetrating wounds from cats and dogs may need stitching by a veterinarian and/or antibiotic treatment to prevent wound infection.

Prevention Avoid feeding wildlife on the ground where they may be vulnerable to cat and dog attack. Put several bells around the cat's collar and provide lots of safe hiding and perching places for birds in your garden.

Dehydration

Dehydration can be a problem in injured birds. They may have suffered the injury some time before being rescued and may not have had food or drink for days. Oral fluids will help to rehydrate the bird quickly. These can be given by tube directly to the crop (part of the gullet) or stomach. For birds such as parrots, which could bite through a plastic tube and swallow it, a crop needle is used. A crop needle is a metal tube with a smooth bulb at the end. These can be attached to a syringe so the dose can be measured. Feeding tubes are used for all other birds. Feeding tubes and crop needles are available from veterinary surgeries.

Fluids are given to the crop of birds that have a crop (all seed-eating birds) and to the stomach (called proventriculus) of those birds without a crop. When inserting the tube, care must be taken not to damage the oesophagus. The tube must be moderately soft and pliable and not have any sharp edges. Be sure you are familiar with the anatomy of a bird's mouth (see page 114) before you attempt to tube-feed. The feeding tube or crop needle is passed over the back of the bird's tongue and inserted into the oesophagus. Two people are usually needed to tube-feed a bird—one to hold the bird and one to give the fluids. Restrain the bird gently as holding it tight will cause it to struggle even more. Gently straighten the neck. Pass the tube slowly, allowing the bird to swallow as the tube goes down. If the tube is in the right place you will be able to feel it as it moves down the oesophagus. Don't inject any fluid until you are sure the tube or crop needle is in the correct place. Administer the fluid slowly.

The volume of fluids given varies with each species but a general guide is given below. Fluid can be given until it can be seen welling up in the back of the throat. The tube is then gently removed and the bird given the opportunity to shake its head to discard excess fluid. Oral fluids such as Lectade or Vy-trate can be given at a rate of 1–2mL per 100 grams of bird weight. Oral fluids can be given three to four times daily until the bird is rehydrated.

Average volumes that can be used for birds are as follows:

Bird weight	Dose rate
50 grams	0.5–1mL
100 grams	1–2mL
150 grams	1.5–3mL
200 grams	2–4mL

Many birds obtain much of the moisture they need from their food. It is essential to provide all injured or sick birds in care with water in a dish. Water dishes should be suited to the type of bird they are intended for. Many bird species scoop water with the lower mandible (jaw) and then tilt the head backwards so the water runs down the throat. The dish should be deep enough to allow a bird to do this.

Hygiene risks

It is important to maintain a very high standard of hygiene at all times, particularly if more than one bird is held. The stress caused by injury, capture and captivity may predispose birds to further illness.

Did you know that ravens and currawongs often attack small caged birds?

These birds often kill young or small birds through the bars of the cage in which they are housed. Make sure the cage is large enough so the young bird can get away from a potential attack through the bars. Cover three-quarters of the cage with a towel or similar so the young bird feels secure.

The potential to spread of disease from one bird to another or to humans can be minimised with good hygiene and husbandry practices. Make it a daily practice to wash food and water containers and clean out enclosures and aviaries. Remove all uneaten food daily and scrub water containers then fill them with fresh water. Regular cleaning of food and water containers, perches and cages with a mild disinfectant, such as household bleach, will help prevent the spread of any diseases.

Food and water containers should never be placed under perches as the bird will urinate and defecate in the dishes. Food and water in aviaries should be placed under shelter to prevent droppings from wild birds contaminating the caged animal.

Before examining large seabirds, the beak should be secured by holding it shut. Take care not to cover the nostrils.

> ### Did you know that you can return a baby bird to its nest after it has fallen out?
>
> Popular belief has it that adult birds will reject young that have been handled by humans. However, smell is not as well developed in most bird species as it is in mammals and it is unlikely that the parent birds would smell that the youngster had been touched by humans.

Care for specific bird groups

Waterbirds

Handling seabirds It is risky to handle seabirds, such as albatrosses, which have strong beaks. Before trying to carry out any examination, the beak should be secured. The external nostrils of some birds, such as cormorants, Darters, gannets and pelicans, are almost non-existent. These birds mostly breathe though the sides of their bill. When securing the bill, hold it firmly but allow the bill to open slightly so the bird can breathe. With all other birds, take care not to cover the nostrils as this will stop the bird from breathing. Some species will also scratch severely with their feet. A net or thick towel may be a useful catching and restraining tool.

Herons, egrets and Darters catch prey with a fast, stabbing motion. They may defend themselves by stabbing at your face or eyes. Immobilise the bill by holding it securely. Wear protective goggles and hold the bird away from your face.

Handling swans, ducks and geese Swans can break a human's bones by striking with the 'wrists' of their wings. Their wings must be secured before handling them further, both to protect the handler and to avoid damage to the bird from excessive flapping. Hold the wings and, once they are immobilised, fold them in their natural position against the body, then the bird can be held under one arm.

Handling wading birds Wading birds include stilts, dotterels and plovers. No special handling technique is required for most wading species. However, care must be

Ducks and geese can be handled by folding the wings against the body to prevent the wings from becoming damaged due to excessive flapping.

taken not to injure the legs of some long-legged species and the fragile bills of many waders. These birds can be handled as shown on page 87 for insectivorous birds.

Temporary accommodation Many waterbirds are not accustomed to being on their feet on abrasive surfaces for lengthy

periods. The tender flesh of the feet could become sore, cracked and infected on concrete or a similar surface. A very slippery floor, such as bathroom tiles or lino, may cause muscular or ligament damage. These problems may be prevented by keeping the bird on grass or by covering the floor with rubber matting, which cushions the feet and can easily be kept clean. Sand works well provided it is spot-cleaned, raked daily and changed regularly.

A pond must be provided if the bird is kept for more than 24 hours. Many waterbirds are accustomed to preening (grooming) while in the water. Unless water is provided, the bird could lose the waterproof condition of its feathers. It could then become waterlogged or drown when released into water.

A perch may need to be provided for some species, such as herons, and some form of cover, for example some leafy branches hanging over the water, would also be appreciated by most birds.

Wading birds should not be kept in a small cage as this may cause injury to their delicate legs or to the bills of long-billed species. Unless a large cage or aviary is available—lined, for example, with shadecloth—these birds may be housed in a large cardboard box. Flywire or similar may be draped over the top to provide security.

Feeding Most seabirds, such as gannets and penguins, can be fed on whole fresh fish—Whitebait, Red Spot Whiting or Yellowtail. Tinned fish should not be used. Match the size of the bird to the size of the fish, that is, Whitebait for terns, whiting for gannets. Very sick or weak birds should be given small fish, such as Whitebait, until they regain some of their strength.

Initially, waterbirds may need to be force-fed, a job that will require two people (see the section on force-feeding, page 118). One person wraps a cloth around the bird to prevent it from flapping and gently opens the bill, with or without leather gloves, depending on the sharpness of the bill. The second person can then slide a fish head-first down the throat and gently stroke the neck to facilitate swallowing. With patience the bird may be taught to take fish from the hand or from a dish.

Ducks and geese may be fed lettuce, bread, chopped lucerne, clover, cabbage, spinach, chicken or turkey pellets, as well as grain such as cracked corn and wheat. The food should be placed in a dish of water as most of the animals in this group feed off the surface of the water rather than from a dish. If a pond is available to the animal, food can be placed directly into it, provided it is cleaned daily.

A suitable food for wading birds is a mixture of crumbled sponge cake, millet, turkey starter pellets, finely minced meat or canned dog food, grated crumbled cheese and crumbled hard-boiled egg yolk.

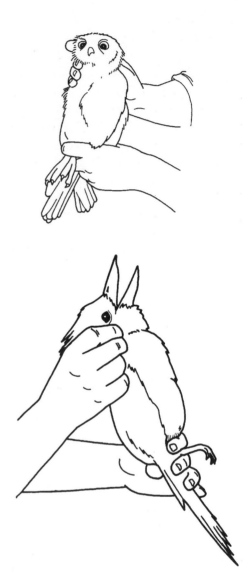

The head and feet of meat-eating birds should be held securely at all times when handling.

Meat-eating birds

This group includes eagles, hawks, owls, falcons, frogmouths, kookaburras, magpies, and currawongs.

Handling Many meat-eating birds have sharp or hooked bills as well as powerful claws, particularly birds of prey, such as owls, eagles and falcons. A towel or cloth should be thrown over the bird prior to handling. The feet of birds of prey should be secured first, then the head secured. Gently fold the wings and restrain them simultaneously to avoid damage from excessive flapping. For birds in the meat-eating group other than birds of prey, such as magpies, currawongs, butcherbirds and kookaburras, the head is secured first, then the feet and lastly, but in quick succession, the wings are restrained. The head and feet must be held securely at all times when handling these birds.

Temporary accommodation The larger birds of prey are best kept in an aviary with large mesh and lined with hessian or sheets to prevent feather damage and must be provided with several solid roosts or perches. Kookaburras, magpies, currawongs and cuckoo-shrikes can be housed temporarily in a 'cocky cage' or small aviary with some cover, such as leafy branches, for security. Kookaburras and magpies can be given a normal size perch, approximately two to three centimetres in diameter, but frogmouths and nightjars like a thick perch on which to roost or sit.

Feeding Hawks, eagles and falcons are birds of prey and should be fed on whole food such as dead mice, rats, rabbits and young chickens. The size of the food should be in proportion to the size of the bird. Initially, injured birds of prey will need to be tempted to eat. This can be achieved by slitting the abdomen of the food and exposing the entrails.

Frogmouths and nightjars seldom feed themselves initially in captivity. When the beak opens in a defence/threat gesture, a small mouse may be dropped in it. If the bird does not swallow this, force-feeding may be necessary (see page 118). The food can be dipped in water prior to force-feeding so that it will slide down more easily. Kookaburras, magpies, currawongs and cuckoo-shrikes can be fed canned dog or cat food or dog kibble soaked in water.

Insect-eating birds

This group includes robins, silvereyes, whistlers, thrushes, flycatchers, fantails and swallows.

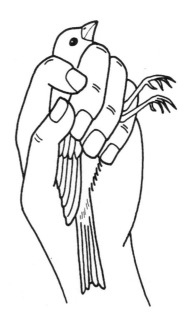

Insectivorous birds are delicate and must be handled very gently. Make sure the bird's breathing is not restricted while being held.

Handling These birds are delicate and must be handled with care. Some might have sharp claws but it is best to handle them with clean, dry and bare hands; serious injury to the handler is unlikely. Little birds should not be handled with gloves, as gloves make it difficult to judge how much pressure is being applied to the bird. It is particularly important not to squeeze small birds or hold them too tightly as this will restrict breathing.

Temporary accommodation These birds can be kept in a small bird cage or cardboard box with a perch. Many are easily frightened and a light cover, such as a tea-towel over the cage, provides more security. If all the light is blocked out, however, the bird may not eat. Some light must enter the enclosure to encourage feeding behaviour.

Feeding These delicate birds should not be force-fed as the stress could be fatal. If the bird is not eating, it can be tempted with live food, such as grubs, worms, moths, crickets and grasshoppers.

A mixture of crumbled sponge cake, grated cheese, crumbled hard-boiled egg yolk, flies, a small amount of canned dog food, grubs, moths and worms should be offered. Insect eaters will also appreciate some nectar mix (see food mixes, page 121). If the bird has not eaten at all for 24 hours, tube feeding may be attempted (see page 115).

Seed-eating birds

This group contains quail, parrots,

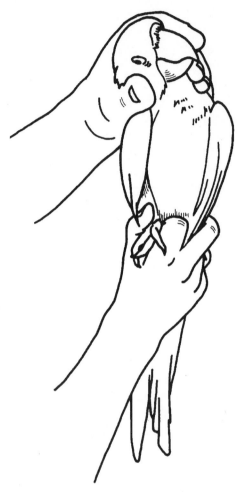

Parrots can inflict severe bites and their head and feet should be held while restraining them.

cockatoos, finches and some pigeons and doves.

Handling As a defence mechanism, many pigeons and doves may produce a shock moult—releasing many feathers in an attempt to deter attackers. Pigeons, doves and quail must be restrained by placing both hands simultaneously around the body and wings to prevent injury caused by excessive flapping. Parrots can inflict severe bites and must be handled in a similar manner to meat-eating birds. Finches are very delicate and must be handled with extreme care.

Temporary accommodation A bird cage is suitable for parrots and a cage or cardboard box is suitable for pigeons and doves, finches and quails. An appropriately sized perch should be provided and the cage or box covered with fly mesh or similar material—if the bird is flighty or nervous, some cover over the cage or box will make the bird feel more secure. Quails in particular will need some leafy branches bunched up in the cage for security, or they can be kept in a cardboard box.

Feeding Pigeons and doves can be fed wheat, cracked corn, millet and turkey starter pellets.

Small parrots such as budgerigars can be fed canary seed, hulled oats, millet, sunflower seed, apple and pear. Medium-sized parrots such as rosellas should be given sunflower seed, oats, millet, cracked corn, wheat, canary seed, apple, pear, lettuce and spinach. Large parrots such as galahs and cockatoos need to be fed sunflower seeds, whole corn, wheat, hulled oats, peanuts, apple, pear, lettuce and spinach. Finches can be fed millet and canary seed.

Honey and nectar eaters

This group includes noisy miners, wattlebirds, honeyeaters and lorikeets.

Handling Honeyeaters can be handled with cloth or thin gloves to prevent their sharp claws from injuring your fingers. Rainbow Lorikeets are renowned for their painful bites so these birds are best handled with thick gloves or a sturdy cloth.

Housing A bird cage or cardboard box with a perch is suitable for most of these birds. If the bird is flighty or nervous, the cage or box should be covered with a cloth or fly netting. Lorikeets, however, will need a small cage as they can chew their way out of a box.

Feeding For honeyeaters, a mixture of one part raw sugar to six parts water, with a small amount of high protein baby cereal, should be provided. An orange cut in half, insects such as grubs, flies and worms, and a small amount of canned dog food are also necessary.

Small honey- and nectar-eating birds can be held gently in the hand. Take care not to restrict their breathing.

Did you know that owls fly at night on large yet silent wings?

They are able to fly so silently because their feathers are covered in a very fine down and the leading edges of the feathers are frayed, which hushes the noise of their wing beat. As they are not fast hunters, they rely on surprising their prey, as they appear without a sound.

Lorikeets should be fed a mixture of one spoonful of raw sugar to 12 spoonfuls of high protein baby cereal (see reference section p. 129), made up with water to resemble a 'porridge' consistency. They should also be fed soft, sweet fruit such as apple, pear, banana, pawpaw and orange cut in half.

Fruit eaters

This group includes figbirds, bowerbirds, orioles and some pigeons and doves.

Handling Some of these birds have sharp claws and should be handled with a cloth or thin gloves. See also the information on pigeons and doves under 'Seed eaters' on page 88.

Temporary accommodation A bird cage or cardboard box with a perch is suitable for these birds. The cage or box should be covered with fly mesh or similar material for flighty or nervous birds.

Feeding Chopped fruits such as apple, banana, pear, pawpaw and grapes should be provided, and a small amount of canned dog meat can also be offered.

Fruit-eating birds can be handled safely if care is taken to secure their claws.

Handling
AND EMERGENCY CARE
OF REPTILES

S ick and injured reptiles are commonly encountered by members of the public and their treatment and care differs considerably from that of the more familiar birds and mammals. Reptiles are ectothermic, or cold-blooded, meaning that their body temperature varies with the temperature of the environment. All bodily functions, especially healing and digestion, are dependent on correct body temperature, so that providing the right environment for an injured reptile is of utmost importance.

Reptiles may take many months to recover completely so the provision of the correct environment during convalescence is important. Handling, housing and feeding is covered briefly here, but for longer term care additional advice must be sought.

Many reptiles are rescued when there is nothing actually wrong with them. On cold mornings reptiles are quite inactive. They emerge in search of some sunshine in which to bask. If left alone, they will soon warm up and move off.

Freshwater turtles are commonly found in and around ponds in parks, blue-tongue lizards are found in gardens and geckos are seen on walls in basements. Such animals have adapted well to these not-so-natural environments and should be left alone.

Did you know that a snake's outer skin is shed from time to time to allow room for growth?

A few days before a snake sheds its skin its eyes start to look cloudy. The skin turns dull and colourless and the snake may lose its appetite. Snakes in captivity are often more aggressive at this time. Water should be provided nearby as the snake loses body fluids along with the dead skin.

Catching and handling

The same principles apply for catching reptiles as apply for other animals. The animal should be caught safely, quickly and gently. However, as some reptiles may be venomous, additional precautions are needed.

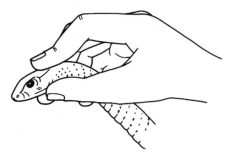

Correct holding position for snakes: firmly but gently hold the head ensuring that the animal's breathing is not restricted, while holding the snake with the other hand. The rest of its body should also be supported.

As a general rule, reptiles are easier to catch when the weather is cold. Try to catch them early in the morning or at night. Avoid catching reptiles in the middle of the day as they are likely to be more mobile.

Handling snakes

Venomous snakes should never be approached—they should only be handled by experienced herpetologists. Reptile rehabilitators should first learn to identify snake species and be positive and confident about their identification. If in doubt check with an expert. Once rehabilitators are confident handlers of non-venomous snakes, they may wish to handle venomous species. The way to handle venomous species must be learned from an experienced herpetologist. One-to-one tuition is needed for as long as it takes for the experienced herpetologist to feel confident that the learner is qualified to handle venomous species.

Snakes can all be handled in a similar manner. The head is immobilised with a suitable tool, such as a padded forked stick called a 'jigger'. The snake is then grasped firmly behind the head with one hand. The other hand supports the body and tail. To transfer the snake into a bag, continue to hold it behind the head while placing it into the bag. Then grasp the snake behind the head with the other hand from the outside of the bag. Once the snake is held firmly through the outside of the bag, the hand inside the bag can be withdrawn and the bag closed securely.

Handling lizards

There are no venomous Australian lizard species but some groups, such as monitors (goannas), can bite and scratch severely. Monitors should be handled with thick leather gloves. The head is restrained around the neck and shoulder region, followed quickly by restraining of the back legs. Face the legs away from your body to avoid scratches.

Although some captive monitors are handled by the tail, never be tempted to catch a wild monitor by the tail. The animal can swing around easily and bite.

Small lizards can be netted or encouraged to walk into a shelter from which they can be caught. Larger monitors can also be netted but there is a possibility that they will rip the net and escape more agitated and aroused than before.

Many skinks and geckos can drop their tails voluntarily as a defence mechanism. Take care to handle these lizards gently and never pick them up by the tail. Cup your entire hand over the animal then carefully firm your grip around it. Alternatively, a towel can be thrown over the animal before it is picked up.

> ### Did you know that the shell of a turtle is living tissue, just like our bones?
>
> Some people who keep a turtle as a pet drill a whole in the shell so the turtle can be tethered. This is very painful for the animal. There is also a great risk of infection by drilling into living tissue.

Handling turtles

Most freshwater turtles are easily handled by the shell. Grasp them firmly around the shell and keep the head pointing away from you. Turtles can spray a foul-smelling secretion from glands at their back end. Hold the turtle away from you to avoid these secretions soiling your clothes.

Large marine turtles will need to be carried by more than one person as they can weigh several hundred kilograms. Take care not to have hands and fingers too close to the mouth of a turtle as they can inflict severe bites. Turtles should be grasped firmly as they will try to 'push off' with their hind legs. This can cause handlers to lose their grip and drop the animal. Turtle shells will crack if dropped on hard surfaces.

Transport

Reptiles can be transported successfully at a consistant temperature of approxi-

mately 20°C. A variety of methods may be used for different reptile groups, as follows. (Note: do not leave animals in closed vehicles.)

- freshwater turtles—use a ventilated box to fit the size of the animal or a cotton bag for short distances
- marine turtles—transport on top of thick rubber (10cm) to protect the shell. Do not enclose it in anything. May need to be transported in a truck. Keep shaded and cool
- geckos and skinks—use a ventilated box or cotton bag
- land snakes—a cotton bag should be used (but put a venomous snake in its bag inside a ventilated box to prevent bites through the bag)
- sea-snakes—use a large water container, such as a plastic garbage bin, one-third filled with water, if the animal is conscious. If unconscious, transport in a ventilated box or bag.

Housing

It is critical to provide reptiles with the correct temperature, humidity and light. Temperature is discussed in more detail below. Humidity for reptiles is kept between 35 and 75 per cent depending on whether the animal originates from a tropical, arid or temperate area.

All reptiles should be provided with a water dish large enough to bathe in. Put some pebbles in the dish to weigh it down so it does not get thrown over. Animals from tropical regions are kept in enclosures with lots of dense foliage.

In addition, this foliage is lightly sprayed with water twice daily to increase the humidity. Only the branches should be wet in this process, and excess moisture on the ground should be avoided.

Aim to provide the reptile with its natural 'photo period'. Normal day length and light intensity for the time of year is important in the captive care of reptiles as it stimulates physiological functions. Light also influences the animal's feeding behaviour and it may not feed in dark circumstances. If at all possible, reptiles should be exposed to direct sunlight every day as ultraviolet light helps the animals absorb some essential vitamins.

The cage floor can be covered in either newspaper, soil, fine-grade mulch or dry sphagnum moss. All faeces should be removed immediately to avoid contamination. Cage furniture can be provided, such as climbing structures for tree-dwelling snakes. Ensure these are firmly in place so the animal does not fall or become trapped in the structure.

All reptiles should be given a safe place to hide for privacy. A small cardboard box with an entrance hole or some broken terracotta pots will be sufficient for ground-dwelling animals. Climbing species may prefer a suspended nestbox. Cage furniture will also help the reptile to shed its skin.

Temperature

All reptiles have a preferred body temperature. This is the body temperature that allows the animal to perform at maximum efficiency. Reptiles achieve this preferred body temperature by basking in the sun. Most reptiles, when given the opportunity, will seek out a temperature between 25°C and 32°C, although there are exceptions to this. Digestion of food and healing of injuries is best achieved when the animal is kept at its preferred body temperature. Indoor cages must have a heat source. This can be provided with low-watt globes, from 25 to 100W, or infra-red lights. Light bulbs must always be covered as snakes may coil around them and get burned. An alternative heat source are heat pads or 'hot rocks', which can be bought at pet shops. These heating elements are set in plastic or concrete and are pre-adjusted to the correct temperature for most common reptiles. The heat source should be placed at one end of the enclosure to create a heat gradient so that the animal can move closer to or further away from it as required.

Some preferred body temperatures for common species are as follows (these are approximate temperatures determined from field and laboratory studies):

- long-necked turtle, 26°C
- Diamond Python, 29°C
- Common Tree Snake, 32°C
- Water Python, 34°C
- blue-tongue lizard, 28–32°C
- Bearded Dragon, 35–39°C
- Lace Monitor, 35°C.

Always have a thermometer in the enclosure and check temperatures regularly. A built-in thermostat will make sure the enclosure does not overheat.

Specific problems

Fractured shells

Long-necked turtles that frequently cross roads are often found with cracked shells as a result of car accidents and sometimes dog attacks. Usually only the shell is damaged but it is also possible that one or more limbs are broken.

It is a fallacy that a fractured shell can be glued back together, covered by fibreglass and the animal released immediately. It is simply not the case. The shell of a turtle is living tissue—it is bone covered by scales. Fractured shells must be treated by a veterinarian as one would deal with a fractured limb. The veterinarian will take X-rays of the animal, clean the wound and remove any dead or infected tissue. If no infection occurs, the shell may eventually be repaired with fibreglass. In some cases it may be necessary to wire bone fragments together to promote healing. First aid consists of transporting the animal to a veterinarian as soon as possible.

Ticks

Blue-tongue lizards are often seen with large ticks on their bodies. These reptiles are not affected by the paralysis-inducing ticks as are dogs, cats and humans. If a reptile is seen to have a tick it will not need to be caught. The tick will fall off the animal once it is fully engorged. Only heavily infested reptiles, particularly if they have ticks in their ears and eyes, should be caught and taken to a veterinarian to have the ticks removed.

Cat and dog attacks

Lizards such as blue-tongues, shingle-back skinks and water dragons are prone to cat and dog attacks. The wounds must be treated by a veterinarian. Meanwhile keep the animal quiet and insulated against temperature fluctuations.

Temporary accommodation

A few basic necessities must be provided for all reptiles. A heat lamp, such as a 100W lightglobe, should be placed in one end of the enclosure and positioned in such a way that the reptile will not come into direct contact with it (see the illustration on page 122). The lightglobe must also be placed to allow for hot spots as well as cold spots in the enclosure. The temperature in the enclosure should be monitored closely with a thermometer to maintain a range of between 25°C and 28°C.

To make the animal feel secure, hiding places need to be provided, and can take the form of a cardboard box, short lengths of ceramic pipe, some large pieces of bark or a hollow log. A small water bowl should be provided and placed away from the heat source.

In general, the enclosure should be kept as dry as possible. However, the rainforest reptile species like a fine, misty spray of water several times a day. Branches for climbing should be given to tree-dwelling lizards and snakes and some rough material, such as sandstone, is useful to help the animal shed its skin.

Feeding reptiles

Wild reptiles can initially be difficult to feed. Digestion in reptiles depends largely on the temperature at which the animal is housed. The temperature must be maintained at optimum levels after feeding. A sudden drop in temperature after feeding may lead to regurgitation or decomposition of the food in the stomach.

Before feeding reptiles it is essential that the animal is housed correctly and the ambient temperature is suitable for the species. A settling-in period for reptiles prior to feeding is not unusual. Snakes in particular may take several weeks before they accept food. Lizards and turtles are usually more willing to accept a diet in captivity.

As with all aspects of captive husbandry, feeding reptiles requires a commonsense approach. To provide a suitable diet for captive convalescing reptiles, take the following points into account:

* obtain or replicate the food that the animal feeds on in the wild
* present food items of a suitable size and presentation
* ensure foods such as insects and snails have not been in contact with any insecticides.

Lizards Lizards have a wide variety of food preferences, as might be expected in a group of animals that differ considerably in their habitat preferences, size and form. Most smaller species are insectivorous so a wide variety of insects, preferably live, should be offered. Some species of omnivorous lizards may also eat clover, dandelion, mulberry leaves, milk thistle, watercress, chopped fruits and vegetables, such as banana, apple, pawpaw, pear, lettuce and tomato, as well as snails and slugs. Small amounts of moistened dog kibble and canned dog food may also be eaten. The insect diet can also be supplemented with Wombaroo reptile supplement.

> **Did you know that young reptiles grow inside eggs with parchment-like shells?**
>
> The young have an 'eggtooth' that they use to slash a hole in the shell to hatch. Some lizards such as blue-tongue lizards and some snakes are 'viviparous', which means they give birth to fully developed young instead of laying eggs.

Blue-tounge lizards will appreciate some live snails and meal worms. If the lizard is rather ill or very injured and convalescing, snails or other live food may be too difficult to deal with. In this case, it can be tube fed with a crop needle usually used to tube feed parrots. Lizards have sharp teeth and may be difficult to feed with a plastic tube.

Feeding frequency is approximately every two to three days. Lizards are active animals with a metabolic rate that is higher than snakes and they therefore require regular, small meals—in warm weather every two days, in colder weather every three days.

Monitors Monitors, or goannas, are carrion feeders and should be fed rats, mice, chickens, fish and canned dog food approximately weekly.

Freshwater turtles are largely carnivorous, feeding on fish, molluscs, crustaceans and tadpoles. Species of the genus *Elseya* (such as the Saw-shelled Turtles) also feed on pandanus and other fruit. In captivity, turtles are offered a variety of natural foods in the water because they rarely feed on land. Uneaten food must be removed immediately to avoid fouling the water.

Foods that can be offered to captive turtles include earthworms, tadpoles, insect larvae, prawns, yabbies and whitebait. Small pieces of lean meat and tinned cat food can also be given. In addition, aquatic vegetation can be offered to short-necked species of turtle.

Freshwater turtles can be tube fed with a crop needle used for parrots. They may clamp down their jaw on a plastic feeding tube making it very difficult to remove.

Vitamin A deficiency is common in young turtles. This can be prevented by providing a balanced, adequate diet. It may be beneficial to provide calcium supplementation by placing a block of plaster of Paris in the water. Small, young turtles should be fed daily, while adults can be fed twice or three times a week.

Foods for marine turtles are not given here because the specialised requirements of these species dictate that they should only be rehabilitated by institutions, such as zoos and aquariums.

Did you know that snakes 'smell' with their tongues?

Snakes flick out their forked tongues to pick up chemical particles in the air or on the ground. The tongue then takes these particles to the roof of the mouth. There, the 'Jacobson's organ' partly smells and partly tastes these particles.

Snakes Snakes are carnivorous predators and should be offered whole prey. Pythons and some other snakes suffocate their prey by constriction while other snakes kill prey by envenomation. Most snakes rely on movement as well as smell to locate their prey. All snakes swallow their prey whole. Snakes can be trained to accept dead prey. Live prey should never be left with a snake as it may cause injury to the reptile. There are reports of newborn, hairless mice being left as food for a snake and gnawing the snake's skin so badly that the snake had to be put down.

If two or more snakes are housed together, they must be separated prior to feeding as they may begin to eat the same prey item, which can lead to cannibalism of one of the snakes. The majority of rehabilitating snakes will adapt quickly to feeding on dead prey. Initially, if needed, freshly killed prey can be used. When using frozen and thawed prey it may be necessary to warm the prey item to body temperature. This can be done in warm water.

Avoid using the microwave oven to reheat thawed out prey items to feed to snakes as the microwave oven does not heat items evenly. The types of food items which can be offered to snakes include mice, rats and day old chickens.

Wriggling the dead rodent in front of the reptile with a long pair of forceps may encourage feeding. If the reptile does not grasp the rodent immediately, leave the prey item in the enclosure for a few hours as the snake may eat it when left undisturbed.

Sometimes snakes will refuse food, even though it seems that all environmental requirements have been met. Periods of fasting are common in snakes and, provided the animal is not emaciated, it may choose not to eat for a couple of months. After that, it may be necessary to consider force-feeding as a last resort.

The ability to take large prey items allows snakes to feed infrequently. A prey item should not exceed five to ten per cent of the snake's weight. If the animal has not eaten for some time it is probably better to offer small prey initially. A suitably sized prey item would create a slight bulge in the snake's mid section.

For most snakes a weekly or fortnightly feed is sufficient if the meal is of adequate size.

Hand-rearing
ORPHANS

The previous chapter dealt with the emergency care of injured mature and immature animals. In many cases, however, you may find an uninjured orphan, commonly associated with the death or injury of a parent or separation from the parent through misadventure. Orphaned animals are very fragile, highly stressed and need as much attention as you would give an injured animal. Without immediate and appropriate care, their health may deteriorate rapidly.

This chapter gives general guidelines for the emergency care of these orphans. For more detailed information on the longer term care of individual species contact your local wildlife authority (see the reference section, pages 127–8) for a referral to a wildlife rescue group, zoo or fauna park in your area.

Hand-rearing a native animal is enjoyable and rewarding but it should only be contemplated if no other alternative is available. If you know that the animal's parents have been killed, you have the choice of rearing the animal or having it put down. If the animal looks to have been abandoned but you cannot be sure, then there is a chance the parents may return to it.

In the case of a young bird, try to find the nest and put the youngster back. Stay around the area (unobtrusively) for a while and watch out for the parents. If they return to the nest, there is good reason to believe that they will continue to care for their offspring.

In the case of a young possum, try to return the animal to its mother. At dusk, the young can be placed in a basket in a tree near where it was found. The mother can be attracted to the site by playing tape-recorded calls of her young. Stay around to ensure that the taped calls do not attract predators. If the mother makes contact with her young she is most likely to continue to care for it.

Only when you are quite sure that the animal has been orphaned or permanently abandoned should you take it home.

The first step in caring for an orphan is to keep it warm and quiet. Once it has settled down, check it gently for injuries and decide whether it needs veterinary attention.

The next step is to identify the youngster and find out all you can about the species. Useful books to learn more about the species should be available at local libraries and bookshops. The reference section also lists organisations where further assistance can be obtained (pages 127–8).

The third step is to give careful thought to whether you are able to rear the orphan. Consider the following questions:

◆ do you have the facilities needed, for example, a cage, aviary, garden, pet blanket, electric blanket, and so on?

◆ can you care for the animal? That is, are you willing to feed it three-hourly, or more often, and during the night if needed? Are you at home all day and, if not, can you take the animal to work (provided it is quiet there)?

◆ can you provide the food it needs, for example, live insects, worms, mice, eucalypt leaves?

◆ will it be safe from marauding pets? Can you keep your neighbours' pets as well as your own away from the animal?

◆ are you able to pay veterinary costs?

◆ are you willing to make a commitment for as long as it takes to rear the animal? For some species, such as wombats, this can be as long as eight or ten months.

If you can't answer all the above questions with a firm 'yes', it is better to take the animal to a place where it can be cared for properly. Contact your local RSPCA, the National Parks and Wildlife Service or equivalent, or a local veterinarian to find out where the animal could be taken for suitable care.

General points

In most States you will need a licence from the National Parks and Wildlife Service, or the equivalent organisation, to care for a native animal. State wildlife authorities are listed on pages 127–8. You are also obliged to return the animal to the wild once it is old enough and able to fend for itself.

In hand-rearing an orphan, you have the responsibility not only for its physical care but also for providing it with living skills in preparation for its release into the wild. Living skills for wild creatures include knowing what to eat and where to find it, where to sleep, how to avoid predators and to be cautious of humans. Probably the most important lesson an orphan must learn is that it is not a human—a difficult concept to teach. There are, however, some tricks that can be employed. For example, birds can be fed with a glove puppet resembling an adult bird over the hand so that the captive bird has a model on which to mirror itself. Never cuddle animals that do not need it. Marsupial joeys and orphaned bats need physical contact and thrive on it but must be weaned off this human attention to make them grow more independent. Birds and reptiles, on the other hand, need food and warmth but not cuddles. In fact, the less they are handled, the better their chances of surviving after release back into the wild.

Stress

Stress is one of the most common causes of death in hand-reared animals. The triggers for stress are difficult to predict—what causes stress in one species is not necessarily a problem for another species. To avoid stress in an orphaned animal, try to duplicate as closely as possible the conditions it would encounter with its mother. This usually means a quiet environment, so taking the animal on public transport in peak hour, or to the school playground, could be very stressful. Forcing a marsupial out of the pouch before it is ready is also stressful and should be avoided. The animal will explore the world when it is ready to do so and should not be forced. Too much handling, in particular by strangers, is also distressing for most orphans. Handling, feeding and cleaning the animal should be carried out preferably by the same person or by as few people as possible.

Some animals are very prone to stress. Hand-reared ringtail possums, for example, often suffer from a condition called 'stress alopecia'—they lose their fur due to stress. (Fur loss can also happen if the animal is kept too warm.)

Stress can be recognised and alleviated by getting to know the animal, observing it closely and noticing differences in its stress levels. Many animals utter stress calls when upset. These calls are different in every species but a keen foster parent will soon become familiar with the sound.

Company

It is essential that an orphan's foster parents find it another animal of the same species for company. Local veterinarians, voluntary wildlife organisations or the RSPCA may be able to put you in touch with another person who is rearing a joey or a bird of the same species in your local area. The orphan needs some social contact to develop skills. More importantly, it needs to learn to recognise its own species. When seeking a mate in adult years it needs to recognise potential partners. When an opportunity arises for your orphan to live with another orphan of the same species, take it. Their survival chances after release will be greatly increased.

Hygiene

Hygiene is a very important factor in hand-rearing orphans. Before feeding or handling bottles, wash your hands thoroughly and sterilise all bottles, teats and other equipment between feeds. If more than one animal is being reared, wash your hands between feeding or handling each animal.

Fresh food must be prepared daily and stored in the refrigerator. The artificial nest or pouch must be kept scrupulously clean with any old food or faeces removed immediately. Young animals are prone to infections and cleanliness may save their lives.

Feeding

Marsupials are lactose intolerant. That means they cannot be fed with products containing cow's milk. Cow's milk can cause anything from diarrhoea to blindness in very young joeys. If you are unsure what to feed the orphan, contact a local veterinarian, wildlife rescue group or zoo for advice. Diets given in this book are of a general nature and are adequate to maintain animals for two to three days. For care that extends beyond that time, the animal may require additional vitamins, nutrients and variety. Young animals grow very quickly and must have the correct diet to cope with rapid development.

Hand-rearing marsupials

Marsupials are mammals whose young are born at an undeveloped stage. The offspring climbs into the mother's pouch after birth where it develops further. Kangaroos, wallabies, wombats, possums, bandicoots, Koalas and gliders are all marsupials.

Artificial pouch

Young orphaned marsupials need an artificial pouch in which to feel secure. The size of the pouch depends on the size of the animal and needs to fit it fairly snugly. Only natural materials, such as cotton and wool, should be used to make artificial pouches as synthetics are often too hot or too cold and do not 'breathe'. Ideally, a cotton pouch liner should be used inside a wool pouch, which will help to keep the joey warm. Older animals can use synthetics but take care as some joeys may suck the pouch and synthetic fibres can damage the gut if swallowed.

A sock makes an ideal pouch for very small possums, such as ringtails and Sugar

Only natural materials like cotton and wool should be used to make artificial pouches. This Yellow-bellied Glider is kept warm in a woollen beanie.

gliders. A handtowel sewn up on two sides, perhaps inside a woollen beanie, makes a good pouch liner for larger possums, such as brushtail possums. An old woollen jumper sewn up at the neck and armholes makes an excellent pouch for kangaroos and wombats. Pillowslips can be used as pouch liners for kangaroos and wallabies.

Always leave the top of the pouch open a little to prevent overheating. This would allow a larger joey to move away from the heat source if it becomes too hot inside the pouch.

Warmth

Young marsupials are often cold when they are found. If the animal's feet feel cold its body temperature will be low.

The animal must be warmed slowly, for example, by placing it under your clothing wrapped in a pillowslip. Pouch young must be kept at a constant temperature. Animals with fur all over the body can be kept at about 28°C. Naked or unfurred joeys must be kept warmer—at about 34°C to 35°C. Very young orphans need external heat to help them maintain a constant temperature. A heat source can be provided by an electric blanket on its lowest setting, animal heat pads, foot warmers or hotwater bottles. Baby animals can easily become overheated, which can often be fatal. Temperatures must be monitored with a thermometer inside the pouch, beside the joey, at all times. If the electric blanket or foot warmer is too hot, layer some towels on top until the correct temperature is achieved. Hotwater bottles should be used only as a last resort as they cool down fast. Small animals cannot maintain their own body temperature well so it is important that a constant heat source is provided.

Dehydration

Small marsupials are often suffering from dehydration when first found. Some animals may have lost their mother a number of days before being rescued and may not have suckled for some time. To check for dehydration, pinch the animal's skin at the shoulders between your thumb and finger. If the skin stays 'peaked' for several seconds, the animal may be dehydrated. If the skin springs back immediately, the animal is well hydrated. (Test your own skin's reaction by pinching the skin on the back of your hand, then compare it with a test of the animal's skin—if it springs back similarly to your own, it is well hydrated.) If dehydration is suspected, the animal may benefit from veterinary assessment. It may require an injection of rehydration fluids under the skin or, in severe cases, directly into the bloodstream. For mild cases of dehydration, oral rehydration fluids such as Vy-trate or Lectade may be given. These products are available from veterinary clinics.

Hygiene

Cleanliness is essential when rearing joeys. Lack of hygiene leads to infections, which could easily kill the animal.

Yeast infection (thrush) is often caused by poor hygiene. The animal must be thoroughly cleaned after each feed. Spilt milk, urine or faeces must be washed off the fur with moist cottonwool and dried with paper tissues. Carers should wash their hands before and after each animal is handled.

Particular attention should be paid to the area under the chin as many orphans develop a dermatitis infection in this spot caused by milk left on the fur. Matted fur allows dirt to be trapped and should be combed gently with a toothbrush and thoroughly washed. These animals should not be bathed but gently 'sponged' with moist cottonwool or cloth and dried with tissues or a soft towel.

Bottles, teats, syringes and other feeding implements must be sterilised after each feed using a baby-bottle sterilising agent, available at supermarkets or chemists.

Pouches must be scrupulously clean. Joeys should never be left in a soiled pouch, just as a human baby should not be left in a dirty nappy. If the animal is toileted (see page 107) after each feed, soiling of the pouch should not occur often. Pouches can be soaked in a commercially available nappy-wash then machine washed. Disposable nappies are an alternative, but are expensive.

Feeding orphaned marsupials

Young animals should only be fed when their body temperature is correct. If the animal has just been found and is cold, ensure that is gently warmed up before it is fed. The milk formula should be fed to the animal at body temperature, which ranges between 35°C and 37°C. There are several artificial milk substitutes available for orphaned marsupials. When choosing a suitable milk substitute, the availability of the product may be a consideration. Once a joey has started to drink a particular marsupial milk formula it may be unwise to change it as any change may cause intestinal upsets. Discuss with the local veterinarian which milk product is suitable for the joey and whether it is easily obtained in your area. A list of products and addresses is given in the reference section (pages 129–30).

Water for making up the milk formulas should be boiled for 10 minutes and cooled before use. The milk formula can be divided in daily batches and frozen until needed. Reconstituted milk should be kept in the refrigerator and discarded after 24 hours. Remember the following rules:

- ensure the animal's body temperature is correct before feeding
- never reheat milk
- store prepared milk formula in the fridge
- wash bottles and teats immediately after use.

Emergency formula for unfurred marsupials

For the first 24 hours, a newly orphaned animal can be fed on a solution of 100mL boiled water and one teaspoon of glucose. This also allows for a transition period from a maternal milk diet to the artificial diet. Feed formula at body temperature, approximately 35° C.

Frequency of feeding

Feed unfurred animals approximately every two to three hours and furred animals approximately every four hours. Frequency of feeding must be adapted to suit the individual orphan. Some orphans, particularly those who are weak or dehydrated, will initially need more frequent feeding. Feeding more often than at two-hourly intervals is not recommended as the youngster will tire easily and weaken further.

How much to feed

The amount of milk formula a joey must receive every 24-hour period is related to its body weight and may vary depending on the formula chosen. Most marsupial joeys are adequately fed if they drink between 10 and 20 per cent of their body weight in formula every 24 hours, and no more than 20 per cent of their body weight in a 24-hour period. For example, a joey that weighs 1kg (1,000g) must drink between 100 and 200mL of formula daily. A small possum that weighs 100g must drink between 10 and 20mL of formula daily.

When the animal starts to eat solid food, its intake of milk can be decreased slowly over a period of weeks and water can be given in a bowl.

Teats

Marsupial teats differ in size and shape from those used to feed human babies or domestic animals. The size of the teat is very important. If the teat is too big or too small the joey will not get a good grip on it and will have trouble drinking.

The illustration below shows a number of commercially available teats and the animals for which they are suitable. The hole in the teat must be small and can be made by piercing the teat several times with a hot needle. Particularly for small joeys, it is important that the flow of milk is not too fast. If too much milk enters the mouth at once, the joey will not be able to swallow fast enough and some milk may be inhaled. The inhaling of milk can be fatal as it may cause pneumonia. The flow of milk is too great if milk can be seen bubbling out of the joey's nose. This should be avoided at all costs. Milk inhalation can also be prevented by holding the joey on its side so that milk can run freely out of the mouth.

An emergency teat can be made from an eye-dropper or a small syringe with a valve from a bicycle tyre attached to it. Alternatively, use a syringe with a gastric feeding tube or 'cat catheter' attached to it, or an intravenous catheter (available from veterinary surgeries). If a valve or tube is used, ensure that it is attached very securely so it will not come off and be accidentally swallowed. It could be attached with a small electric cable tie.

Feeding method

Young joeys are best kept in the pouch while bottle-feeding them. The first few feeds might be troublesome as the milk formula tastes different from maternal milk. Some perseverance is required. The milk should never be forced down and, as mentioned previously, the flow of milk should not be too fast—that is, the hole in the teat must not be too large. If the joey chokes on the milk or bubbles come out of the nose, the flow of milk is too great.

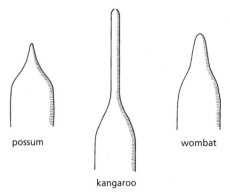

possum

kangaroo

wombat

Marsupial feeding teats.

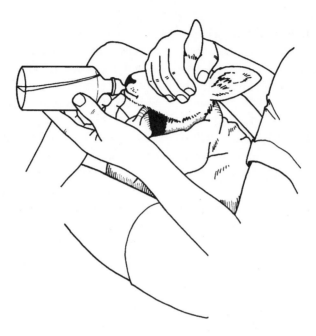

Joeys usually feed best if their eyes are covered during feeding. They are then less likely to be distracted.

It may be necessary for the first few feeds to insert the teat in the joey's mouth. Gently open the animal's mouth with your thumb and forefinger and insert the teat. Joeys usually feed best if it is dark, quiet and there are no distractions—as if in the mother's pouch—so try covering their eyes with a hand during feeding.

Feeding solids

The time to start feeding solids is indicated by Mother Nature—when the joey has teeth it is meant to use them for chewing solid food. Generally the youngster is also fully furred at this stage. The introduction to an adult diet should be gradual: small amounts of food can be given in the pouch, such as a little grass for kangaroos and wombats (make sure this is fairly dry, older grass rather than fresh grass, which may cause diarrhoea), and native flowers, leaves and fruit for possums and gliders. The joey can leave the pouch for short periods at this point and, to encourage this, small amounts of food can be given outside the pouch.

The milk formula should be given in decreasing amounts while the animal is being weaned to its adult diet. It is important to weigh the animal regularly—three times per week is recommended—during the entire hand-rearing period and especially at this time. Any weight loss may indicate that the reduction of milk has been too rapid and more should be given. Weaning in marsupials, especially in macropods, is prolonged compared with placental mammals and should not be rushed.

Toileting

A marsupial mother licks the joey's anal area to stimulate urination and defecation. The joey may become constipated or develop kidney problems if it is not stimulated to urinate and defecate. You can imitate this by gently rubbing its genital area with a moistened tissue or cottonwool. Do this after each feed until weaning. When the faeces' consistency changes from paste to pellets, the joey can be put on the ground to urinate and defecate.

Toileting an orphaned marsupial.

Exercise

A very small orphaned joey does not need much exercise as in nature it is in its mother's pouch continually. As it grows older, becomes fully furred and starts to eat solids, the joey must be given the option of leaving the pouch when it wishes. It should never be forced to play or stay out for long periods because this will stress the animal. However, it may be encouraged to come out of the pouch for short periods. To do this, place the pouch in such a way that the animal can enter and exit freely, and put some titbits just outside the pouch, such as grass for kangaroos and native flowers for possums.

Once the animal is eating a reasonable amount of solid food—half its food intake—extra opportunities for exercise must be provided, for example, a yard for kangaroos or an aviary with climbing structures for possums. Initially some exercise can be given in half-hour sessions, slowly increasing as the animal grows older and becomes more confident. At this stage the animal may still need some additional heating on cold nights with a pet blanket or other form of heating. An animal eating solely solid adult foods should be put in a yard or enclosure as detailed in the section on emergency care in Chapter 5.

Hand-rearing flying foxes

Bats are placental mammals (eutherian), like us. They are different from marsupials in that they give birth to well-developed young and do not have a pouch. For the first few weeks, the young flying fox hangs on to its mother with its wings, feet and mouth and she supports it with her wing.

Species identification

Species identification of bats can be difficult. Small insectivorous bats are often mistaken for baby flying foxes. There are two groups of bats: microbats (mainly insect eaters) and megabats (mainly fruit and nectar feeders). An easy way to tell the difference is by examining their eyes.

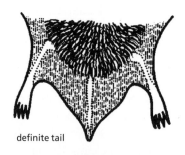

definite tail

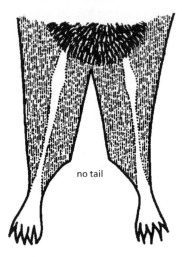

no tail

Fruit-eating bats have no tail while insectivorous bats have a definite tail.

Flying foxes have large, round eyes while the insectivorous bats have very small eyes, the size of pinheads. Another quick method of determining if a bat is from the insectivorous or the flying fox group is by the presence or absence of a tail, as shown in the diagram on this page.

Once you have identified the group to which the bat belongs, it is easier to further identify the particular species and to care for it. Baby insectivorous bats are seldom found. They weigh only a few grams at birth and probably go undetected if they fall to the ground. The main type of orphan bat that people are likely to encounter is the flying fox.

Housing

For very young flying foxes some carers use a 'mumma'—a 'pretend mother' flying fox. A mumma is made by folding a handtowel in half and then rolling it into a cylinder. Use a flannelette or cotton cloth to cover the handtowel. A tissue may be placed over the area where the animal will be urinating and defecating. The animal then snuggles onto this and is loosely covered with a cloth. The wrapping must be loose so the animal can move out of it when it wants to. The animal can then be placed in a basket or pet carry-box on layers of soft towelling. The young flying fox is most comfortable when placed at a 45° angle with the head down.

At approximately three to four weeks of age the young bat can be housed in a bird cage or similar. This should be large enough for the animal to stretch its wings

Very small flying foxes can be wrapped up loosely to provide warmth and security.

freely. A cloth should be attached to one wall of the cage for the bat to hold on to. At this stage the young bat will sleep either on or wrapped up in some cloth. Continue to wrap the animal loosely onto its mumma after each feed but in such way that it can unwrap itself. At approximately three months of age the bat must be given an aviary or large enclosure where it can practise making short flights. It is very important that the bat has access to sunlight. This helps to prevent fungal infections of the wings and is essential for the development of the young bat.

Warmth

Additional heating is needed for young bats up to six weeks of age. This can be provided by a heating pad, electric blanket, or hotwater bottle. Care should be taken not to overheat the animal. Allow the animal to regulate its temperature by moving either closer to or away from the heat source. The animal should not be wrapped too tightly—it must be able to regulate its own temperature.

Hygiene

A very young bat is unable to clean itself and this job is usually done by its mother. By the time the bat starts to hang independently for most of the time it will also keep itself clean. Until this time, the foster parent needs to wash the bat daily. This can be done with a warm sponge bath similar to the way a bedridden human patient is washed in hospital.

Particular attention must be paid to areas under the wings. Bats are prone to fungal and bacterial infections of the wings if this area stays moist or dirty. After the bath, the bat should be dried by patting it gently with a towel.

Feeding implements must be disinfected after each feed, using a baby-bottle steriliser, available from chemists or supermarkets.

The bat's wrapping cloths must be changed as soon as they are soiled, soaked in a nappy-wash disinfectant solution and then washed normally.

Feeding orphaned flying foxes

Milk formulas suitable for flying foxes are available through chemists and veterinarians. Some are listed in the reference section (see page 129). The amount of milk formula the bat

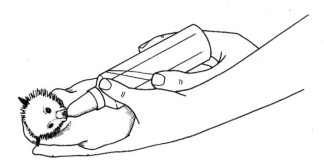

While feeding a young flying fox it should be on its side with the head slightly lower than the rest of the body so that any excess milk can drain out of the mouth.

must receive every 24-hour period relates to its body weight. Fruit bats are adequately fed if they drink 10 to 20 per cent of their body weight in formula in a 24-hour period. For example, a bat that weighs 100 grams must drink between 10 and 20mL of formula daily. Bats up to four weeks old should be fed three-hourly. After four weeks, with body weight 150 g and over, feed them four-hourly.

Young bats are best fed with a bottle and teat. The formula must be heated to body temperature, approximately 35°C. During bottle feeding, keep the animal wrapped securely and lying on its side. The head should be slightly lower than the rest of the body so that any excess milk can drain out of the mouth easily. It is essential that the flow of the milk from the teat is not too fast because milk can be inhaled and cause death. If the bat chokes on the milk or bubbles come out of the nose, the flow of milk is too great.

Feeding solids

Solid food can be introduced to the young bat at approximately seven weeks. Small amounts of pureed fruit can be given in addition to the milk formula (see the reference section, pages 129–30, for product names). When the bat gets older, the amount of pureed fruit should be increased and the milk intake decreased. For example, cut out one milk feed first and, if the bat's weight still increases, cut out another milk feed while increasing the fruit. Weigh the bat three times per week during the entire hand-rearing period and particularly during the weaning period.

At about ten weeks of age, small pieces of fruit sprinkled with Complan or Wombaroo can be offered in addition to the pureed fruit and the milk intake can be decreased further. When the animal is approximately five to six months old, it should be fed completely on chopped fruit comprising mainly apple and sprinkled with a tablespoon of Complan or Wombaroo. In addition, eucalypt flowers, native figs and lilly-pilly fruits can be offered.

Exercise

Exercise is important because the bat cannot be released unless it can fly well. Very young flying foxes less than three weeks old do not need much exercise, but they should have their wings unfolded and folded several times a day to exercise their muscles. From three weeks onwards, the bat should be given enough room to stretch its wings and hang on a cloth. If the animal hangs comfortably for short periods it should be given the opportunity to flap its wings freely.

At about three months of age the flying fox must be given regular access to an aviary, one with high wooden perches and large enough for short flights. The walls of the aviary should be 'padded' at first to soften any crash landings. Towels and leafy branches can be used.

Hand-rearing birds

The first step is to identify the bird and find out more about the species' specific needs. If these needs can be matched in captivity, the stress on the bird will be reduced. Identification of nestling birds is difficult but searching the internet for photos of baby birds of the most likely species may help.

Accommodation

Tiny birds are best kept at 35°C. Warmth can be provided with a suspended lamp or an adjustable desk lamp with a red lightbulb, an electric blanket at its lowest setting, a pet heating pad, electric frying pan, a heat lamp or hotwater bottle. Constant temperature is important for very small birds but this is difficult to achieve using wrapped hotwater bottles as they cool quickly so they should be the last option. The temperature must be monitored closely by observing the animal and with a thermometer. A bird that is too hot will pant or breathe with an open mouth. A bird that is too cold may be shivering or, if more than one bird is kept, they may be clustering tightly. Extreme fluctuations of temperature are often fatal to little birds and must be avoided at all times.

Very young birds—naked or downy—can be kept in an artificial nest made from an empty ice-cream container or a cane or plastic basket lined with a piece of towel and a top layer of tissue paper. For birds that perch it is beneficial to provide some small sticks in the nest that they can grip with their claws. For chicks of

Artificial nest made from cane basket lined with towelling and tissues.

hollow-nesters (birds that nest in tree-hollows such as kookaburras and parrots), some untreated sawdust can be placed in the nest. This prevents malformation of the legs as the chick grows. The nest can then be placed in a cardboard box. Darkness is important to encourage sleep and rest. Sleep deprivation can result in stunted growth in very young chicks, particularly in chicks of hollow-nesters.

Some species, such as most ducklings, will appreciate a feather duster suspended just above the floor level of the enclosure. They can snuggle into the safety of this environment, which mimics the effect of being under a parent.

Juvenile birds (feathered) will need some space and can be kept in a cage. The cage should be large enough for the bird to flap its wings freely—it needs to do this to build up the muscles necessary for flight. Once the bird shows signs of wanting to fly, it must be given a flight aviary for practice.

Unless a bird can practise flying it will not stand a chance in the wild. It may be good at flying short distances but its muscles will tire very quickly if it is chased by another bird. The demands of catching or collecting food requires plenty of stamina and the bird must be prepared for that.

The aviary or cage must be fitted with a number of perches. Perch preferences are an individual thing and different species like different perches. The main point to remember is to make sure the perch is a good fit for the bird's foot. Perches in flight aviaries should be placed in such a way as to allow the bird to fly from one end to the other. Flight aviaries should be long enough for birds to circle in flight, and perches can be placed across corners. While the bird is learning to fly, some leafy branches may be used to line the aviary to provide a soft landing.

Flight aviary with perches at either end. The outside aviary should have shelter from sun, wind and rain on three sides so that the bird is protected from weather extremes.

Feeding baby birds

Adult birds feed on an enormous variety of foods and the same food sources are usually used to feed their offspring. An exception are pigeons, which produce milk in their crop (part of their digestive tract) to feed their young.

By identifying the species of orphan you are caring for, you can ascertain the diet for the adult bird. The adult diet may have to be adapted to suit young birds; for example, if the adult bird eats whole fish this would have to be blended for the orphan. The fish porridge can then be given through a syringe and tube. In order to obtain a suitable diet for the orphan, you may have to contact a State wildlife authority for information (see the reference section, pages 127–8).

The following is an emergency diet which can be fed to nearly all young birds until the correct diet is known. Soak commercially available dog kibble in cold water. When the kibble is soft right through, it is ready to be used. Squeeze out any excess water as this may cause diarrhoea. Do not give food that is icy cold—this may reduce the body temperature of the bird. Give food at the bird's body temperature, which is about 39°–40°C. Feed only small amounts at a time but feed regularly throughout the day when the bird begs for food.

It is important to weigh the bird regularly to ensure its food intake is adequate. Healthy young birds will show a slow but steady weight increase until they reach adult weight.

Feeding methods for baby birds

Baby birds can be divided into two groups in terms of development at hatching. One group—precocial—is well advanced at hatching and is covered with downy feathers. The other group—altricial—is less developed at hatching and is naked and helpless.

Precocial chicks are well advanced at hatching and are covered with downy feathers.

When altricial chicks hatch they are naked and helpless and are dependent on their parents to supply food.

Feeding precocial birds

Precocial birds include ducks, geese, chickens, Mallee Fowl, emus and plovers. These birds feed themselves from the start whereas a newly hatched bird will usually not feed for at least 24 hours. Place the appropriate food (see diets, pages 119–121) in a flat feeding bowl and encourage the bird to feed by tapping your finger in the dish, pretending that your finger is another bird's beak and is taking food. A few live meal worms added to the food bowl, available from pet shops, will create movement, which can encourage the chick to feed. Alternatively, you could obtain a hen or some young chicks to show the young bird what to do.

A shallow dish of water must also be given but not one that is deep enough for the chick to drown in. The water dish should also be non-slippery as the chick could slip over and drown, or sustain tendon damage. Placing small clean stones in the dish will help to avoid the chick drowning or slipping.

Feeding altricial birds

Altricial birds include kookaburras cockatoos, lorikeets, parrots, magpies, finches and currawongs. These are birds which hatch naked and helpless, do not feed themselves initially and are dependent on their parents supplying food for the first part of their lives. When hand-rearing a bird of this type, feeding must be done regularly throughout the day, giving small amounts each time. A strong healthy chick can go throughout the night without food. Very young chicks, however, may need feeding regularly from about 6 am to 11 pm. Ensure that the bird is comfortably warm before feeding. The correct body temperature for birds is approximately 39°C.

A hungry chick will gape (open its mouth wide) to encourage the parents to feed it. The gaping reflex in young birds is usually activated when one of the parents lands on the nest. A touch on the side of the improvised nest will usually make the chick gape. Sometimes a gentle tap on the side of the bill or at the base of the lower bill in parrots will help gain a feed response. Feed as often as the bird gapes, but small amounts only.

If the bird is removed from the heated box for feeding, place it under a desk lamp with a red lightbulb or similar to prevent

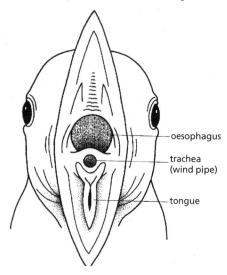

The anatomy of a bird's mouth.

chilling. Loss of body temperature reduces the feeding response in chicks.

When feeding baby birds, the utmost care must be taken to ensure no food or fluids end up in the bird's glottis—the opening to the windpipe. The anatomy of a bird's mouth is very different from that of a human mouth. In birds, the opening to the windpipe is situated just behind the tongue, in front of the oesophagus, which is the tube that the food goes down. If the bird takes the food itself from tweezers, a stick or fingers, it will know to close the glottis before swallowing. However, if the bird is being 'force-fed' by syringe or with fingers, care should be taken to place the food well beyond the glottis.

Syringe feeding

This is necessary for chicks whose parents regurgitate food for their young. The syringe can be extended with a soft tube (feeding tubes and syringes are available from veterinary surgeries). This method can be used for very small or very weak birds that cannot be spoon-fed. Ensure the tube is a tight fit to avoid it coming off and being swallowed by the bird. The tube may be attached to the syringe with a very small electric cable tie.

Beginners may need assistance to syringe-feed a chick, while more confident bird handlers can probably manage alone. When inserting the tube, care must be taken to prevent possible damage to the oesophagus and crop. The tube must be soft and pliable and not have any sharp edges. Before attempting

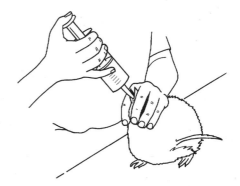

Syringe-feeding is necessary for chicks whose parents regurgitate food for their young.

to syringe-feed, study the figure on the previous page and learn to recognise the features in the chick's mouth. You will then be able to avoid putting food down the bird's windpipe. When finished feeding, pull the tube out very slowly as feeding tubes removed too quickly can cause a 'vacuum effect', bringing food back up.

Not all birds have a crop, although most seed-eaters do. This organ is used as a storage area where seed can be softened before going further down the digestive tract. Care must be taken not to overfill the crop. If it is too full, food will be brought up and may be inhaled down the windpipe, which can be fatal. Start by giving small birds that need syringe-feeding no more than 0.1mL of food. If taken easily, increase the amount slightly according to the size of the bird.

Prior to each feed, the crop must be felt to ensure that it is empty or almost empty before more food is given. The crop should empty out completely at

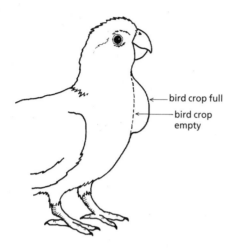

bird crop full

bird crop empty

Take care not to overfill the bird's crop.

Spoon feeding

This method can be used for a chick that feeds on regurgitated food from its parents. Bend a teaspoon with a pair of pliers so that it resembles the parent's bill. Feed the chick by inserting the first part of the spoon into its beak. The bird will suck the substance off the spoon and swallow it. Many birds fed by this method will continue to beg for food when the crop is full, therefore the feeder must keep an eye on the crop, as described for syringe feeding, and stop feeding when the crop is distended. Ensure that the food is given at body temperature.

least once every 24 hours. The crop should feel completely empty in the morning before the first feed of the day. If the crop does not empty overnight this could indicate a problem and a vet-erinarian should be consulted. To understand how to recognise a full or empty crop, feel the bird's crop (see above) before its first feed, and again after feeding.

To feed young pigeons, the end can be cut of a syringe to allow the animal to suck the contents out of the syringe. This simulates the natural chick feed-ing method as they push their beaks into their parent's throat to suck pigeon milk.

Wipe all spilt food off the bird with a moistened tissue on completion of feed-ing as old food can cause infections. Slowly wean the bird to spoon-feeding, or to the bare-hands method, as the bird grows bigger and stronger.

When spoon feeding, bend a teaspoon to resemble the parent's bill. Feed the chick by inserting the first part of the spoon into the bird's beak.

Slowly teach the chick to feed itself by lowering the spoon into a dish with its food and then withdrawing the spoon. This may take several weeks.

Wipe the bird clean with a moistened tissue after each feed.

Eye-dropper feeding

This method of feeding is risky as food can be inhaled. However, for some chicks, such as small finches, it is often the only way to feed them. Prior to feeding, make sure you fully understand the anatomy of a bird's mouth (see page 114). Feed only very small amounts at a time

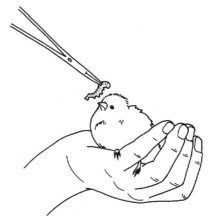

Tweezer feeding.

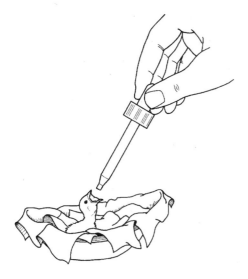

Feed only very small amounts at a time when using an eyedropper.

and change to feeding from tweezers or a matchstick as soon as possible. Feed only when the bird is gaping and stop feeding when the gaping looks less vigorous.

Tweezer feeding

Use plastic or wooden tweezers with blunt edges because steel ones with sharp edges or points may damage the bird's mouth. Pick up food with the tweezers, dip it in water to make it slide down more easily, shake off excess water and deposit the food at the back of the chick's mouth. Repeat until the gaping looks less vigorous.

Stick feeding

A wooden skewer or matchstick can be used for this method. Make the point of the feeding stick blunt as a sharp point may injure the chick. Put some food on the end of the stick, dip it in water and deposit the food at the back of the bird's mouth. Stop feeding when the gaping looks less vigorous.

Stick feeding.

Bare-hands method

This method usually works only on larger birds, such as magpies, kookaburras and currawongs. The food is picked up with the fingers, dipped in water and deposited at the back of the bird's mouth. Cease feeding when the gaping becomes less vigorous.

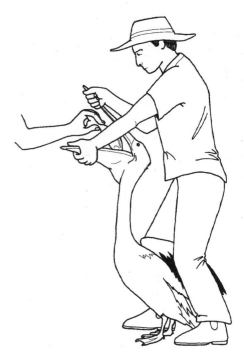

Force feeding: gently open the bird's mouth and place the food at the back of the mouth past the opening to the windpipe.

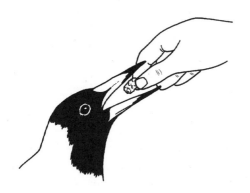

Feeding by hand.

Force feeding

Occasionally a stressed or weak bird may refuse to take food from its rescuer. It may be necessary to force feed the bird several times until it can be encouraged to accept food. An experienced bird handler may be able to force-feed a bird unassisted, but a beginner will need help to carry out this task.

Prior to force feeding, familiarise yourself with the features in the bird's mouth (see page 114) to avoid allowing food to enter its windpipe. While one person holds the bird securely, but not tightly, the other person can gently open the bird's mouth. Small amounts of food, dipped in water, can then be placed at the back of the mouth. If the food is not swallowed, it can be pushed gently down the bird's throat with a finger. Do not use force or sharp objects such as sticks to push the food down because this may cause damage.

Self feeding

As the chick develops into a fledgling—that is, a young bird with full feather development—the time comes for it to learn to feed itself. This can be assisted in several ways. Natural food for the species should be provided in the cage, for example, live insects and grubs for insect eaters, nectar-bearing flowers for nectar feeders and grass seeds for finches. Young birds will play with this and will eventually discover that it tastes good.

When feeding the young bird with tweezers, a stick, fingers or a spoon, hold a food dish under the bird's mouth and pick up food from the dish with the feeding implement. It will eventually discover where the food comes from.

As the bird increasingly feeds itself, hand feeding can be slowly decreased. The food intake must be maintained at the same level as before. Around the time that the bird has full primary (wing) feathers, it must be weaned to an adult diet. To prepare the bird for release, it is important that it recognises and eats its natural food. It must also have the skills to obtain that food in the wild. A young figbird must learn to pick the figs off the branch. A kookaburra must learn to catch live food. The hand-rearer must take the place of the parent bird and teach the chick to find and eat its natural food. Without these skills the young bird has a poor chance of survival after release. Birds of prey need these food-catching skills to a greater extent and therefore the rehabilitation of birds of prey is best left to specialist organisations.

Food for orphaned birds

Birds can be broadly divided into the following six groups based on the types of food they eat in the wild:

- insect eaters
- nectar and fruit eaters
- seed eaters
- meat eaters (rodents, birds and reptiles)
- fish eaters (crustaceans and whole fish)
- grazers.

A diet and method for feeding each one of the six groups is given below. Note that some species of pigeons and doves are seed eaters and some species are fruit eaters. It is important to identify the animal correctly so the appropriate food can be given.

Insect eaters (robins, silver-eyes, whistlers, thrushes, flycatchers, fantails and swallows):

- egg cake mix (see food mixes, page 121)
- flies, pupae, grubs, worms
- a small amount of nectar mix for the first few days to give extra energy.

Method: tweezers or stick method.

Nectar and fruit eaters (Noisy Miners, wattlebirds, honeyeaters, Rainbow Lorikeets and some pigeons and doves):
- nectar mix (see food mixes, page 121)
- chopped soft fruit, such as banana, pawpaw, ripe pear and grapes
- fine meat mix (see food mixes, page 121)
- flies, grubs, crickets and fly pupae.

Most nectar feeders (honeyeaters and wattlebirds) will also take insects, therefore these should also be given.

Method: tweezers or stick.

Seed eaters (parrots, finches, some pigeons and doves):

+ high-protein cereal mix (see food mixes, page 121) or a commercially available parrot-rearing mix available from pet shops.

Wean to adult food by adding soaked, small seed to the cereal mix at fledgling age. (Soak the seed in water for 24 hours then rinse.) In addition, soaked seed and grasses bearing seed are given to encourage the chick to feed itself.

Method: with pigeons and doves, such as Crested Pigeons, bronze-wing pigeons and Peaceful Doves, syringe-feed the very young ones then progress to a spoon and then to a dish. With parrots and cockatoos, spoon-feed then progress to a dish. For finches, such as Zebra Finches, Double-barred Finches and Red-browed Firetails, use the eye-dropper method then progress to a dish.

Meat eaters (kookaburras, magpies, ravens, crows, currawong, butcherbirds, kestrels, eagles and owls):

+ meat mix (see food mixes, page 121)
+ chopped mice, rats, day-old chicks

(including fur and feathers for roughage once the bird is feathered).

Method: tweezers and stick for smaller species, bare hands for larger species. Progress to teaching the bird to feed itself.

Fish eaters (herons, gannets, albatrosses, pelicans and penguins):

+ whole fish blended with a small amount of water
+ whole fish for the slightly (feathered) older birds. Start with whitebait and increase the size of the fish for the larger species.

The types of fish that can be given are Whitebait, Yellowtail or Red Spot Whiting. Never use tinned sardines or other tinned fish or fish sold as bait. The fish must be fresh and fit for human consumption.

Method: syringe feed very young ones only and progress to whole fish, white bait initially. Whole fish must be fed head-first otherwise the fish's spines could damage the bird's throat.

Grazers (swans, most ducks and geese):

+ poultry pellets or chick starter pellets (available from stock and station suppliers)
+ seed such as cracked corn, millet, wheat and oats—these are fed in a dish with water
+ greens such as lettuce, spinach, sprouts, clover, duckweed and grass.

The greens must be chopped very finely for young birds because large pieces of vegetation could cause a blockage in the bowel.

The prepared pellets are higher in protein than is appropriate for the long-term needs of these birds. For longer term feeding, it may be preferable to provide rabbit pellets (crumbled), which are lower in protein. Too much protein in the diet of these very fast-growing birds can cause deformities of legs and wings. To avoid too rapid growth, restrict their access to pellet food to three feeds of about 30 minutes per day, while unlimited access is given to a fresh supply of chopped greens. Diving ducks, such as the pink-eared duck, must also be given some fine-meat mix (see food mixes, below).

Food mixes

Nectar mix
1 part honey
6 parts water
$1/2$ part Irradol-A (available from pet shops and veterinary surgeries)
Mix all ingredients well.

Fine-meat mix
100g finely minced meat
40g crushed dog biscuits
2 hard-boiled eggs
Mix the ingredients together well until all the meat is crumbly and in small pieces.

Egg cake
400g sponge or Madeira cake (available from supermarkets), crumbled
150g fine-meat mix (see earlier)
4 grated hard-boiled eggs
1 heaped tablespoon fly pupae (if available)
pinch calcium carbonate
Mix all ingredients well.

High-protein cereal mix
1 part honey
6 parts high-protein baby cereal
enough water to make a porridge with some consistency
Mix all ingredients well.

Hand-rearing reptiles

Young reptiles are generally quite able to fend for themselves. Occasionally, however, an injured young reptile may need to be cared for. Newborn or newly hatched reptiles often have substantial food reserves and may not eat for the first couple of weeks of life. If they don't feed within four weeks there may be something wrong with the captive environment. Check temperature, humidity, light and other husbandry aspects discussed in the previous chapter. At this stage you may also need to review the food you are offering the juveniles and attempt to obtain food that mimics the natural food more closely.

All newly born or newly hatched reptiles need access to direct sunlight so they can grow and develop correctly. Sunlight should be direct and not through glass or plastic. Some notes on the requirements of common groups of reptiles are given below.

Freshwater turtles

Young turtles need a tank that will hold enough water so they can swim. An area of 'land' should also be provided: this can be in the form of a rock or a patch of sand above the water level that they can climb onto easily.

Sunlight and diet both play an important role in the development of a strong shell. The tank should be placed in direct sunlight but have a shaded area as well. If the tank can't be placed outside, the animal should be given another small enclosure in which it can sun itself each day for at least an hour. Shade should also be provided. Sunlight should be direct as the benefits of sunlight do not transfer well through glass. Ensure that the outside enclosure is predator-proof.

The diet should consist of prawns, yabbies and pieces of whole fish, and these must be fed to the turtle in water. The tank water should be changed after each feeding or all uneaten food removed as leftover food in the tank may be a health risk to the animal.

Lizards

Youngsters in this group, such as blue-tongue lizards or Shinglebacks, can be kept in an aquarium with additional heating (see notes on emergency care for reptiles, page 95). The diet is similar to that of adults but is offered in much smaller pieces and more often. The addition of

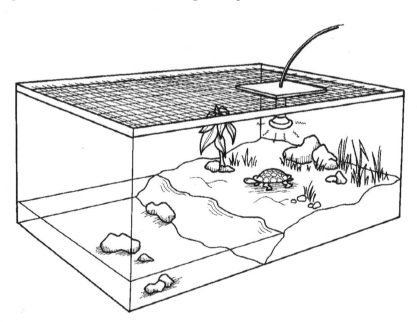

Freshwater turtles need a tank in which they can swim, while some area of 'land' should also be given.

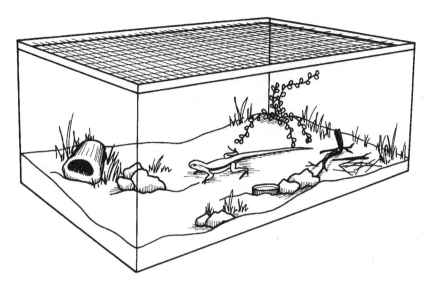

Leaf litter, soil or sand can be placed in the bottom of the tank to allow the lizard to burrow. A hollow log or similar should also be given for shelter.

live insects to the diet will stimulate eating and assist with the development of hunting skills. Water in a dish for drinking should always be available to lizards.

Most lizards will benefit from direct sunlight (not through glass), which helps them develop good teeth and bones. Place the tank outside on sunny days, providing a shady corner and ensure protection from dogs, cats and birds. Leaf litter, soil or sand can be placed in the bottom of the tank to allow lizards to burrow. Stumped-tailed skinks should not be kept east of the Great Dividing Range unless adequate precautions are taken against the effects of high humidity.

Snakes

Prior to handling a snake you must make a positive identification, or seek advice and help from an expert handler. A venomous reptile is venomous at a very early age and can be as lethal as an adult. Venomous snakes should only be handled by experts.

Once you have identified the snake and are positive you have a non-venomous reptile in your care, you can house it in a box or tank with additional heating (see notes on emergency care for reptiles, page 95).

The diet for young snakes is the same as for adults; the size of the food must not be too large for them to swallow. Young snakes can be fed on small lizards and newborn mice. Do not leave live food in the cage or tank because even a small mouse may gnaw at the snake and cause damage while the snake is cold and slow.

Returning wildlife to the wild

The most exciting and rewarding part of caring for any type of orphaned wildlife is releasing it back into the wild. The preparation for release is the most important part in caring for wildlife and should begin the day you start caring for the animal. It must learn to fend for itself, find food, learn to climb, fly, run, swim or whatever it will need to do to survive. The timing for release must be considered carefully. This should coincide with the time the youngster would leave its natural parents in the wild. Whenever possible, more than one orphan of the same species should be cared for at the same time. These can then be released together, providing family support for each other.

Checklist prior to release

- has permission for release been given by the relevant wildlife authority?
- can the animal feed itself?
- does it know and recognise its natural food?
- can it catch live food, if that is what it does in the wild?
- has it been acclimatised to outside temperatures?
- can it fly, run, climb, swim or whatever it needs to do to survive in the wild?
- does it have knowledge of its predators?
- has it had experience with others of its own species?

- does the animal object to human handling?

If the answer is a wholehearted 'yes' to all the above questions, the animal is ready for release. For further information on release, read the section on release in Chapter 4 (pages 59–61).

Release techniques

Two release methods are recognised:

- hard or direct release is release with out support and is mostly used for rehabilitated adults that have spent only a short time in captivity
- gentle, gradual or soft release is when support is provided.

For most hand-reared animals, except perhaps reptiles, soft release is the appropriate technique.

The support given during soft release substitutes, to a degree, for the support the animal may have had from a parent or family group. Support given during soft release may consist of a release paddock for kangaroos and wallabies or an aviary for possums, gliders and birds. This should be located in a suitable habitat for the animal and near its original encounter site. The animal spends some time here in a protected situation prior to release. The animal will become as used to the area at the time of release as would local resident animals at the release site.

The release aviary or paddock is left open for the animal to come and go as it pleases. In the soft release site, the animal will continue to find food and shelter for as long as it needs it. Other support given to, say, a possum or glider may be a nest-box in bushland adjoining the soft release site with a feeding platform nearby. This may help the animal find somewhere to live without having to evict another possum. Birds released from an aviary can be fed for some time in the release site to ensure they have time to develop the skills to find their own food. Most released animals will decrease the amount of food taken from the soft release site after a few weeks. It is then time to reduce the amount of food provided for the animal so it learns to be fully self-sufficient.

Reptiles will benefit from being released at a site that has plenty of shelter. Hollow logs and lengths of clay pipe under bushes and grasses will provide shelter from extreme weather and safety from predators.

Stay around and watch the animal you rescued take its freedom. It is wonderful and satisfying to see the animal return to where it belongs. Enjoy the experience.

Wildlife
AUTHORITIES

The legal requirements for holding native fauna vary from state to state. A permit to hold an injured native animal, even temporarily, will be required in most cases. The addresses and telephone numbers of the relevant wildlife authorities in each state are listed below. The government authorities will provide general advice on wildlife and refer you to a local veterinarian or wildlife rescue group for further assistance.

Australian Capital Territory
Environment, Planning and
Sustainable Development Directorate
Street address: 480 Northbourne Avenue,
Dickson, ACT 2602
Postal address:
GPO Box 158, Canberra City, ACT 2601
Telephone: 13 22 81
www.environment.act.gov.au

New South Wales
National Parks and Wildlife Service NSW
Locked Bag 5022, Parramatta, NSW 2124
Telephone: 1300 361 967
www.nationalparks.nsw.gov.au

Northern Territory
Parks and Wildlife Commission of
the Northern Territory
Telephone: (08) 8999 4555
www.nt.gov.au

Queensland
Department of Environment and Science
GPO Box 2454, Brisbane, QLD 4001
Telephone: 13 74 68
www.des.qld.gov.au

South Australia
Department for Environment and Water
Ground Floor, 81–95 Waymouth Street,
Adelaide, SA 5000
Telephone: 8204 1910
www.environment.sa.gov.au

Tasmania
Tasmanian Parks and Wildlife Service
GPO Box 1751, Hobart, TAS 7001
Telephone: 1300 827 727
www.parks.tas.gov.au

Victoria

Department of Environment, Land, Water
and Planning
PO Box 500, East Melbourne, VIC 8002
Telephone: 136 186
www.delwp.vic.gov.au

Western Australia

Department of Land Management
and Conservation
8 Davidson Terrace, Joondalup, WA 6027
Telephone: (08) 6364 7000
www.epa.wa.gov.au

Products
AND MANUFACTURERS

Biolac
Telephone: (02) 4637 6626;
Mobile: 0406 501 595
www.biolac.com.au

Marsupial Feeding Teats
Telephone: (08) 9291 9795
www.kimani.com.au

Milk Products
Di-Vetelact
PO Box 496, Vaucluse, NSW 2030
Free call: 1800 336 547
www.divetelact.com

Wombaroo Food Products
PO Box 151, Glen Osmond, SA 5064
Telephone: (08) 8391 1713
www.wombaroo.com.au

Other products

Pure fruit baby food (e.g. Heinz 'apples')
Free call: 1800 037 058
www.heinz.com.au

Glucodin
Available in most pharmacies

Sustagen
Available in supermarkets and pharmacies
www.sustagen.com.au

Further action
— CONSERVATION GROUPS

Australian Conservation Foundation
Level 2, 1 Buckingham Street, Surry Hills,
NSW 2010
Free call: 1800 223 669
www.acf.org.au

Australian Wildlife Conservancy
Street address:
Level 2, 322 Hay Street, Subiaco, WA 6008
Postal address:
PO Box 8070, Subiaco East, WA 6008
Telephone: (08) 9380 9633
www.australianwildlife.org

BirdLife Australia
Telephone: (03) 9347 0757
www.birdlife.org.au

The Conservation Council ACT Region
Street address:
Unit 14, 26 Barry Drive, Ground Floor,
Lena Karmel Lodge, Canberra, ACT 2601
Postal address:
GPO Box 544, Canberra, ACT 2601
Telephone: (02) 6229 3200
www.conservationcouncil.org.au

Environment Centre NT
Street address:
Unit 3, 98 Woods Street, Darwin, NT 0800
Postal address:
GPO Box 2120, Darwin, NT 0801
Telephone: (08) 8981 1984
www.ecnt.org.au

Conservation Council SA
111 Franklin Street, Adelaide, SA 5000
Telephone: (08) 8223 5155
www.conservationsa.org.au

Conservation Council of WA
2 Delhi Street, West Perth, WA 6005
Telephone: (08) 9420 7266
www.ccwa.org.au

Conservation Volunteers Australia
Telephone: (03) 5330 0200
www.conservationvolunteers.com.au

Friends of the Earth
Street address: 312 Smith St, Collingwood,
VIC 3066
Postal address:
PO Box 222, Fitzroy, VIC 3065
Telephone: (03) 9419 8700;
Toll free: 1300 852 081
www.foe.org.au

Greenpeace Australia Pacific
Street address:
Suites 4.7 and 4.8, 822 George Street,
Chippendale, NSW 2008
Postal address:
GPO Box 2622, Sydney, NSW 2001
Free call: 1800 815 151
www.greenpeace.org.au

Queensland Conservation Council
1/377 Montague Road, West End, QLD 4101
Telephone: (07) 3846 7833
www.queenslandconservation.org.au

The Rainforest Information Centre
C/– Post Office Elands, NSW 2429
Telephone: (02) 6550 4481
www.rainforestinformationcentre.org

The Wilderness Society
Street address:
174 Charles Street, Launceston, TAS 7250
Postal address:
GPO Box 716, Hobart, TAS 7001
Telephone: (03) 6331 7488
www.wilderness.org.au

WWF Australia
Street address:
Level 1, 1 Smail Street, Ultimo, NSW 2007
Postal address:
PO Box 528, Sydney, NSW 2001
Telephone: (02) 8228 6800;
Free call: 1800 032 551

Photographic credits

Cover

Front cover photograph: Shutterstock | Eric Isselee. Back cover photograph: Shutterstock | Flash-ka.

Colour section

Daroch Donald, photographs 4, 11, 12, 16; Pavel German, photographs 1, 2, 10, 24, 25, 26; Derek Spielman, photographs 5, 6, 7, 13, 14, 15, 17, 18, 19, 20, 21, 22, 23, 27, 28, 29, 30, 31, 32, 33, 34; Rick Stevens/courtesy *Sydney Morning Herald,* photograph 9.

Every effort has been made to trace and acknowledge copyright, but in some cases this has not been possible. The publisher apologises for any accidental infringement of copyright and welcomes information to redress the situation.

Index

ant control 8

bandicoot 4
  basic needs 14
  emergency care for 66–7
  garden, in 45
basic needs 14–16
bats
  emergency care for 73–4
  how they see 56
  roosting box for 29
behaviour, effect of feeding on 22
biological pest control 7
birdbath 23
birds
  avoiding running over 39
  babies
    feeding 113–19
    returning to nest 76, 84
  bacterial infections 79
  dehydration 82–3
  diseases of 78–9
  emergency care 75–90
  entangled 47–8
  first-aid for, *see* first-aid
  flight aviary 112
  fluids table 83
  food plants for 25
  garden, discouraging from 46
  plovers nesting 46–7
  handling 75–6, 84–90
  hand-rearing 111–21
  feeding methods 113–19

food for 119–21
house, removing from 41
hygiene risks 83–4
introduced species 4–5
parasites 79
rehabilitation of 77–8
roof, in 50
transporting 77
blue-tongued lizard, basic needs 14
Brush Turkey 49–50
bushfire victims, rescuing 55

cars
  helping animals cross roads 38–9
  kangaroos and 37
  victims, first-aid for 53–4
  windscreen, bird hitting 60
catching wildlife 57
  equipment list 58
  birds, for 75
  euthanasia 61
  rehabilitation 58
  birds, of 77–8
  releasing
    orphans 124–5
    preparation for 59
    timing 60
    stress of captivity 58
cats
  cat-proof tree 22, 28
  control of 6

feral 5
cockatoo
  basic needs 15
  destruction by, preventing 43–4
cockroach control 8
currawong
  attack 83
  feeding orphans 118, 120
cuttings, taking 19, 20

dogs, control of 6
dove, basic needs 14
ducks
  handling 84, 85
  helping to cross a road 39

echidna 8
  basic needs 14
  emergency care for 64–5
  helping to cross a road 38
emergency
  kit 37–8
  what to do 51–61
emergency care
  birds, for 75–90
  first-aid *see* first-aid
  mammals, for 62–74
    bandicoots 66–7
    bats 73–4
    carnivorous marsupials 65–6
    echidna 64–5
    flying foxes 72–3

housing sick animals 62
  kangaroos 70–2
  koalas 67–9
  platypus 63–4
  possums and gliders 70
  rodents, native 74
  temperature 63
  wallabies 70–2
  wombats 69–70
orphans, for *see* hand-rearing
environment 1–11
euthanasia 61

feeding wildlife *see also* food
  artificial feeding 20
  baby birds 113–19
  behaviour, effect on 22
  birds, food plants for 25
  cat-proof tree 22, 28
  Rainbow Lorikeet 21–2
  safety 22
feral animals,
  impact on wildlife 5
finch, basic needs 14
first-aid
  airway, establishing an 51
  automobile victims 53–4
  birds, for
    broken limbs 79–80
    dehydration 82–3
    feather damage 80–1
    oil pollution 81–2
    predation 82
    windows, flying into 81
  bleeding, preventing 52
  body temperature,
    maintaining 52
  shock, treatment for 53
  stress minimisation 53
  unconscious animals,
    positioning 52
fishing hook, removing 48
fly control 9
flying fox 43
  basic needs 15
  emergency care for 72–3

fruit trees, damage to 42
  hand-rearing 107–11
  protection of 42
food *see also* feeding wildlife
  chain 3
  needs 14–16
  orphaned birds, for 119–21
  plants 17
  suitable 20–2
fruit bat *see* flying fox
fruit pest control 9
funnel-web spider control 9

garden, unwelcome visitors 44–6
garden insect control 10
garden sanctuaries
  see habitat
glider
  basic needs 14
  emergency care for 70
  hand-rearing 102
goanna 45
  feeding 96

habitat
  basic needs 14–16
  creation 12, 16–17
  definition 2–3
  design 16
  food plants 17
  native plants 18–20
  species for nesting
    birds 33–4
  nesting *see* nesting sites
  planning 16–17
  preservation 12
  shelter for ground dwellers 30
  shelter trees for birds 32–3
  shrubs and trees 16
  vegetation layers 13
hand-rearing 99–125
  birds 111–21
  company 101
  feeding 101–2
  flying fox 107–11
  hygiene 101

licence requirements 100
  marsupials 102–7
  reptiles 121–5
  returning to the wild 124–5
  stress 101
honeyeater
  basic needs 14
  Blue-faced 15
house, removing animals from
  41–2
human safety 56–7

injured animals
  see emergency care
introduced animals 4–5

kangaroos
  cars accidents, and 37, 53–4
  emergency care for 70–2
  emergency kit 37–8
  first-aid 51–3
  hand-rearing 102–7
  feeding 106
  joey, how to save 37
koala
  cars accidents, and 53–4
  emergency care for 67–9
  first-aid 51–3
  name, origin of 4
kookaburra
  basic needs 16
  feeding orphans 118, 119, 120
  food chain 3
  nesting hole of 27

lizard *see also* reptiles
  cat and dog attacks 95
  feeding 96
  handling 92
  hand-rearing 122–3
  removing from house 42
  ticks on 95
  whipper snipper,
    damaged by 48
lopping trees 49
lorikeet

basic needs 16
feeding 21–2
Rainbow 21

magpie
basic needs 16
breeding season 43
feeding orphans 118, 120
food, suitable 43
nest 27
marsupials, carnivorous
emergency care for 65–6
hand-rearing 102–7
monotreme, definition of 8
mosquito control 10
moth and silverfish control 9
mould and mildew control 9

names
animal groups list 12
babies of species 66
his and her table 39
native plants 18–20
species for nesting birds 33–4
nest-boxes 27–30
dimensions table 36
placement of 34–6
roosting box for bat 29
small birds, for 30
swallow nest, platform for 29
tree-dwelling mammals, for 29
waterfowl, for 30
nesting sites
artificial *see* nest-boxes
cat-proofing 22, 28
Common Ringtail Possum 26
kookaburra 27
magpie 27
materials for 31
native plant species 33–4
nest, restoring fallen 58
shelter tree species 32–3
tree dwellers, for 26

observing animals 12

oil pollution 81–2
orphans *see* hand-rearing
owls 90

parasites in birds 79
pelicans 48
feeding orphans 118, 120
penguin 45
Peregrine Falcon 79
pest control 6–11
pesticides, homemade 11
pets
abandoning 5
control of 6
pigeon
basic needs 14
feeding orphans 116, 119, 120
platypus 8
bill 30
emergency care for 63–4
plovers, discouraging nesting 46–7
poisoned animals, rescuing 55
pond 23, 25
how to make 24
possum
basic needs 14
Brushtail 15
cars accidents, and 53–4
Common Ringtail 26
emergency care for 70
fence 40
first-aid 51–3
hand-rearing 102–7
removing from house 41
roof, in 39–40
roses, eating 47
trap 40
tree access 28
predators
introduced species 5
natural 8
victims of, rescuing 54

quoll 65

raven attack 83
recipes, bird food mixes 121
rehabilitation 58
birds, of 77–8
releasing animals
orphans 124–5
preparation for 59
timing 60
repellents, homemade 11
reptiles
accommodation 95
feeding 96–8
handling 91–3
hand-rearing 121–5
housing 93–4
shedding of skin 91
temperature requirements 94
transport of 93
rescuing
bushfire victims 55
car victims 53–4
poisoned animals 55
victims of predators 54
roads
helping animals cross 38–9
saving animals hit by cars 37
rodent, native 74
rodent control 10
rosella, basic needs 15

safety for humans 56–7
safety for wildlife 4–5
cat-proof tree 22, 28
feeding, when 22
shelter *see* habitat
shock, treatment for 53
shrubs in wildlife habitat 16
snail control 10
snake *see also* reptiles
avoiding running over 38
feeding 97–8
garden, in 44–5
handling 92
hand-rearing 123
removing from house 41
stress

captivity, of 58
minimisation 53
survival requirements 3–4
swallow
basic needs 14
garden, in 45–6
nest, platform for 29
Welcome Swallow 31

Tasmanian Devil 65–6
transporting
birds 77
wildlife 57–8
trees
removal of 49
saving animals 49
species for bird shelter 32–3
wildlife habitat, in 16
turtle *see also* reptiles

feeding 96
handling 93
hand-rearing 122
helping to cross road 38
shell
fractured 95
properties 93

unconscious animals,
positioning 52
urban animals, introduced
species 4

vegetable pest control 9
vegetation layers 3, 13

wallabies,
emergency care for 70–2
water, providing

birdbath 23
pond 23, 25
how to make 24
waterbirds
emergency care for 84–6
nest-box for 30
wildlife
catching *see* catching wildlife
corridors 1, 2, 12
definition 2
transporting 57–8
windows, why birds tap on 42
wombat
cars accidents, and 53–4
emergency care for 69–70
first-aid 51–3
wren, basic needs 14